P9-DWE-297

SNOW TRAILS
Ski and Snowshoe Routes in the Cascades

by
Gene Prater

THE MOUNTAINEERS
Seattle, Washington

Library of Congress Card Catalog Number: 75-36434
© 1975 by The Mountaineers. All rights reserved.
719 Pike Street
Seattle, Washington 98101
Printed in the United States of America by Snohomish Publishing Co.
  Snohomish, Washington 98290
Published simultaneously in Canada by
  Mountain Craft, Box 5232, Vancouver, B.C., V6B 4B3

Maps by Richard A. Pargeter except as noted.
Cover photo: Lemah Mountain and Chimney Rock, by Yvonne Prater.
All other photos by the author.

CONTENTS

FOREWORD

Some books are conceived in crisis, written in haste, and published at panic speed. Other manuscripts are the products of personal curiosity — researched, contemplated, and argued at great length, and published at leisure, if at all. Still others are written to fill a specific need at a specific time and place — sometimes, but not always — by a person whose inclination has led him to be a superior authority on the subject.

This book is an example of the third category. As snowshoeing and cross-country skiing grew to be recognized as a sport of more than a few eccentrics, a need arose for information to spread these people out so that they would not trip over each others' skis and snowshoes. The obvious person to write such a book had already spent years researching and experimenting with snowshoeing equipment, testing it in the field, and had written a book based on the results (**Snowshoeing,** by Gene Prater, published by The Mountaineers).

Although specific destinations are listed, the idea behind this book was not to tell someone how to start at point A and proceed to point B, but rather to indicate general areas and let the snow traveler go out and explore for himself. Part of the fun of the game is the sense of discovery, the knowledge that the same landscape may be quite different from last season, last winter, or even since the last storm.

Gene's vast background of knowledge about places to go is tempered with the wisdom of where not to go. The reader may be annoyed by constant reiteration of warnings: "slopes are avalanche-prone," "stable snow is essential for this trip," "be sure snow is firm before crossing chutes," "do not proceed beyond this point unless conditions are good." Winter recreation has certain inherent hazards not found in summer. Gene has been avalanched and knows whereof he speaks.

As elsewhere, so too in the winter backcountry, when population density increases, problems develop. Respect the rights of others to enjoyment of the winter outdoor experience. Get a winter recreational parking permit to pay your share for parking; as more permits are purchased more areas will be plowed and new areas opened to the winter recreationist. Once at the designated area, park carefully, leaving as much room as possible for others. Don't block the exit for others who may have to leave before you.

On the trail, remember that different modes of travel require different types of snow. Skiers depend upon the wax gripping a smooth trail. Only skiers should use ski trails — snowshoers, foot stompers, and dogs, please use parallel trails. Snowmobilers will find co-existence with foot travelers easier if they refrain from ruining their trails and don't hog the road from edge to edge.

In the backcountry, leave as little trace of your passage as possible. Use portable camping stoves for cooking and carry tent, poles, and foam pad for sleeping. DO NOT CUT TREE BOUGHS FOR FUEL OR BEDS. Carry out ALL debris, whether from an overnight camp or day hike. There is no excuse for burying cans and wrappers. Give some thought to disposal of human waste. In winter it cannot be buried under a 6-8 inch layer of topsoil as it should be in the summer. Try to stay away from spots that will be creeks or ponds in summer. Remember that during the next three seasons people will be drinking water from the snow the winter tenter lives in (you may return to the area, yourself).

Plan carefully for each trip, no matter how easy it may be. There should be reserve clothing, food, and other essentials for unexpected problems in the party. An overnight stay in an exposed location with inadequate equipment can be fatal in winter. Be prepared to assist others in trouble if necessary.

Many Americans, mesmerized by movies, TV, and professional athletic events, have become spectators. The popularity of winter outdoor recreation, despite its hazards and difficulties, may reflect rediscovery of challenges, abilities, of self-respect. Truly the rewards are there for those who go and seek them.

PREFACE

Two facets of snow travel have had high priority in my thoughts for many years. Even a first-time snow traveler will quickly recognize these: the **how** and the **where** to use snowshoes or skis in the wonderfully varied terrain of our Cascade mountains.

There are three general types of foot travel on snow: snowshoes, touring or Nordic skis, and downhill skis. Snowshoers, of course, walk all the way, both uphill and downhill. Touring skiers may or may not slide-ski-downhill; many people who use these narrow skis with toe clip bindings do not intend to ski downhill, and avoid routes and terrain where they would have to do so. The third group — those who use flexible downhill skis with bindings which secure the boot rigidly to the skis for downhill control — seek out trips which have downhill runs; this is a part of their outing.

In this book, advice to the reader is minimal regarding which routes are better for each of the three types of snow travel device. Nor are the route descriptions so closely detailed that one carries the book in one hand, moving from point to point as directed in the text. Part of the fun of an outing is finding your own way in untracked snow, rather than walking a trail beaten deep by heavy use. Dick Pargeter's excellent sketch maps, based on his pictorial relief map **The North Central Cascades,** certainly should make up for any shortcomings in written description.

Snow avalanches are a possibility on most hikes in winter. Few routes announce "no avalanche hazard." Be aware of this danger, read

up on it, and stay out of hazardous terrain during heavy snowstorms
and afterward, when warm temperatures release snow slides.

Books particularly useful on the subject are: **Snowshoeing,** by the
author, **ABC of Avalanche Safety** and **Snow Crystals,** by Edward R.
LaChapelle, and **Mountaineering: The Freedom of the Hills,** by the
Mountaineers. U.S. Forest Service publications include **Snowy
Torrents: Avalanche Accidents in the United States 1910-1966** and
Modern Avalanche Rescue.

The snow traveler's etiquette should be as rigid as that of the summer hiker. It is especially tempting to bury garbage, as it is so easy to
do. PACK IT OUT. Snow melts. Wood fires and bough beds are also
uncouth. Carry a liquid or compressed fuel stove and a foam pad.
There just aren't enough trees in popular areas to supply all of the
people who frequent these places.

Yes, winter snow travel is becoming more popular. People are learn-
ing how to adapt to oversnow travel, cold temperatures, limited day-
light hours and the danger of sliding snow.

One of the problems, which is annoying, but not a hazard to life or
limb, is where to park the car. The Washington State Highway Department has eliminated all roadside parking on State routes in winter.

The winter of 1975-76 will be the first with a permit sold for winter
recreation parking in Washington. Money raised through sale of permits — $5.00 at present per year — will be used to plow parking areas
for those who buy them, as well as for licensed snowmobilers. Several
years ago it became law that snowmobiles used on public land be licensed. Part of the money collected helps to pay for plowing of parking
spots. This has eased the problem of where to park for snowmobilers,
but led to a certain amount of conflict with foot-powered snow
travelers. Now the Recreational Parking permit and snowmobile license
both permit legal parking in these plowed spots.

At present, parking permits are sold in most mountaineering equip-
ment stores. Plowed sites for recreational parking permits are Hyak
Exit on I-90, 1 ½ miles east of Snoqualmie Summit, Stampede Pass
Exit 10 miles east of Snoqualmie Summit, Cabin Creek Exit 11 miles
east of Snoqualmie Summit, Smith Brook Road 5 miles east of Stevens
Pass on U. S. 2, Mill Creek Road 6 miles east of Stevens Pass on U. S. 2,
Asahel Curtis Picnic Area about 4 miles west of Snoqualmie Summit on
I-90, and the rest area near Coulter Creek on U. S. 2 about 3 miles west
of Lake Wenatchee Road. These are listed in order of preferences, with
funds from sale of permits to be used for plowing. Others may be added
if enough money is raised by sale of permits.

Many people helped with this book; supplying route information were Jim Wiman (most of the routes from Darrington to Mt. Baker), Chet Marler, Gene Mickle, John Zak, Frank Satter, Tom Lyon, Chuck Hessey, Jack Powell, and Loraine Vandiver. Ward Irwin not only contributed ski routes but also kept the project moving as Mountaineer member in charge of liaison. He is a strong skier who made this snowshoer scramble, especially on steep sidehills. Dick Pargeter's talented hand put strong lines and forceful detail on the maps. Dee Molenaar made available his pictorial relief map, **Mount Rainier National Park,** for routes which it best covered. My wife Yvonne spent uncounted hours typing pages of scrambled manuscript. My writing is the crowbar and sledge hammer category, lacking somewhat in finesse and organization; Peggy Ferber aided greatly in editing; some of the expressions she has included are like lace on the burlap of my descriptions.

And most important is the God of the Bible, who created the mountains which are so attractive to us who walk in them. We should honor the One who made this lovely moutain playground as we rush to spend a few hurried hours in a scene often untouched by human hands. "The heavens declare the glory of God; and the firmament showeth His handiwork." (Psalms 19:1)

November 1975   Gene Prater

Ski touring at the end of the North Fork Teanaway Road.

Chapter 1

WHITE PASS
TO THE COLUMBIA RIVER

The southern portions of the Cascade Range contrast markedly with the North Cascades in several respects, and most obviously in the terrain south of Mt. Rainier. The ridges do not rise as high or steeply above the valleys, and the rocky summit spires and hanging glaciers typical of the North Cascades are not found there. But although forest covers most ridge-tops, and the dominant mountain peaks — Goat Rocks, Mt. St. Helens, and Mt. Adams — are widely separated from each other, by no means can the South Cascades be called gentle.

Commercial timber cutting is the principal activity, but in winter the saws and trucks are stilled and snowcover muffles the land and gives it a rest. Trees range from cedar and alder in wet valleys through Douglas fir and hemlock to timberline species of mountain hemlock, alpine fir and white-bark pine. Other varieties of fir abound, but are difficult for the amateur to distinguish.

Snowcover makes road access difficult; at the 2000-foot elevation there generally is enough to stop most family vehicles. Highway 12 through White Pass is open all winter from Interstate 5 south of Chehalis to junction with U.S. 410 west of Yakima.

White Pass

White Pass is a winter sports center, with an excellent downhill ski facility. Many touring skiers and snowshoers are drawn here by the chairlift access to **Hogback Mountain** (6789') with its lovely view of Mt.

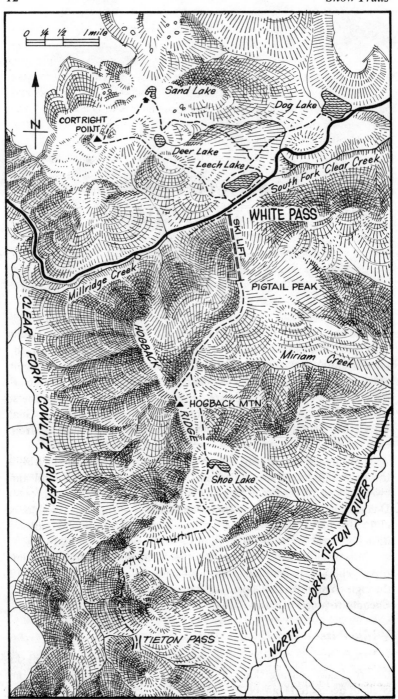

Rainier, Goat Rocks, Adams, and St. Helens. Of all the routes described, Hogback is the outstanding tour for snowplastered timberline trees with scenic mountain backdrop, and it is one of the very few places accessible enough to be reached soon after storms, before the indescribably beautiful rime has melted off. The key is the chairlift ride of 1500 feet elevation to the 5961-foot upper terminal. White Pass Company prefers that snowshoers arrive as early at 8:45 a.m. Sign out at ticket booth or at the upper terminal.

From Pigtail Peak, just beyond the lift, the route is generally on the ridgecrest for 2½ miles to the summit, alternately through stunted trees and in the open. On an especially clear day the Olympics are visible.

Several parties each year camp overnight in this scenic area. Some push on south toward the Goat Rocks and a good campsite at **Shoe Lake** (6100'). Descend off the ridge at the saddle north of Hogback summit to the basin on east if snow on these open slopes is stable (there is usually ample evidence of avalanche activity here) and head south. Climb over the 6600-foot ridge north of Shoe Lake and descend to the lake.

For a longer trip, continue on the Crest Trail route as far as time and energy permit. The trail gradually descends to 4800-foot Tieton Pass, then climbs gently to McCall Basin. Beyond here begin the open slopes of Goat Rocks proper, with Old Snowy Mountain the first high summit. Be sure not to descend off this ridge route into deep canyons of Tieton on the east and Clear Fork Cowlitz on the west; this is one area where following a stream out to a road takes much longer than staying on or near the ridgetop. Skiers can look forward to the downhill run back to White Pass.

North of White Pass is an extensive area ideal for touring and hiking, without much elevation gain or avalanche hazard. However heavy timber somewhat limits the view. About 3 ½ miles from White Pass via the Crest Trail a shelter at **Sand Lake** (5295') makes a pleasant overnight camp. Deer Lake is just off the trail about 2 ½ miles from the pass. Cortright Point (5765') with an excellent view of Rainier, is a mile by trail southwest of Sand Lake. The terrain continues gently for several miles north for a more extended tour.

There are several trips of a mile or so on easy terrain east or west along the lower edge of the White Pass Ski Area. Touring around Leech Lake on the north side of the highway is perfect for less than a full day. If a wide place is plowed for parking at Dog Lake, 1 ½ miles east of the pass, it is possible to explore this area, too (there is no regularly plowed parking space). The more energetic can tour from the pass area to Dog Lake (4207') and return, or be picked up by car at Dog Lake.

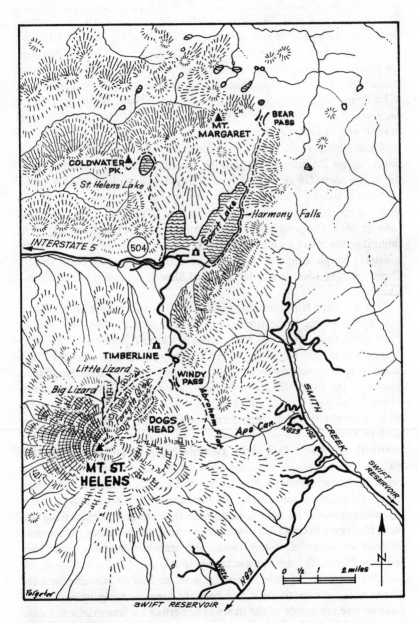

Mt. St. Helens

Mt. St. Helens (9677') is the most accessible of the volcanic peaks in Washington's Cascades. State 504 from I-5 south of Chehalis is plowed to Longview Ski Club near Timberline Campground. The summit

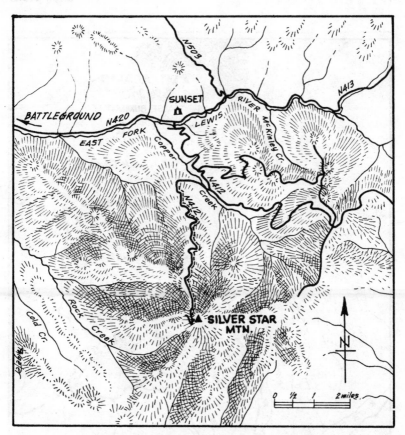

climb is the greatest attraction, although an abundance of touring area is available. Overnight camp can be made at Timberline Campground (4400').

Early or later winter is best for a summit climb, and stable snow is a must; the steep slopes of the mountain are avalanche-prone. A late November ascent has been made on snow soft and deep enough to switchback up the Lizard route on snowshoes to the crater rim, and no avalanches occurred, but generally that depth of new snow on these steep slopes is considered an excessive hazard. When crevasses are solidly bridged with snow, routes can be picked almost anywhere on the slopes above Timberline Camp. The two most popular are Dog's Head, east of Forsyth Glacier, which descends from the crater rim into the canyon west of timberline, and Lizard, west of the glacier. As elevation is gained, Rainier appears over Spirit Lake; Adams is to the east and the Goat Rocks between. From the crater rim the Oregon volcanoes can be seen. The summit is the southwest point of the crater rim.

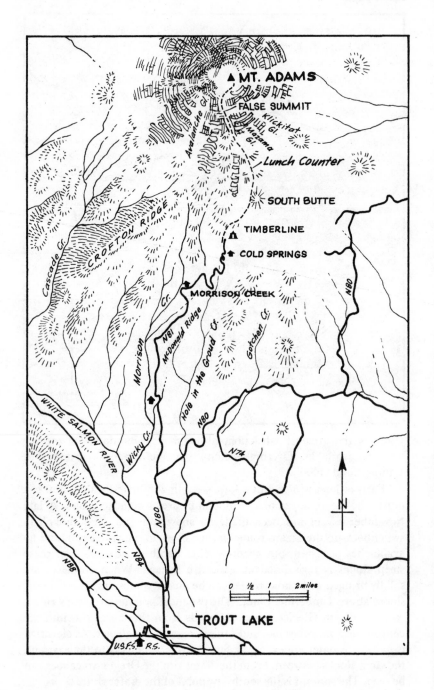

At the east base of the mountain there is a gently rolling area well suited to touring. Shown as **Abraham Flat** or Plains of Abraham on maps, this 4400-foot bench extends nearly 2 miles from Windy Pass (4850') to Pumice Butte at the head of Ape Canyon. It is about ¾ mile from Timberline Camp to Windy Pass.

Coldwater Peak (5727') northwest of Spirit Lake is reached in 5 ½ miles by trail 207 which starts near the lake outlet. St. Helens Lake is reached in 2 ½ miles. The trail circles around the east and north sides of this lovely lake, then climbs about 1 mile to the summit, with a really excellent view of St. Helens.

Several trails follow the east shore of Sprit Lake; trail 211 crosses **Bear Pass** (4905') in 6 miles. The lake shore is excellent for touring; the first 2-3 miles of trail are nearly level. Harmony Falls is reached in 1 ½ miles. The last 1 ½ miles gains 1300 feet to the pass, which overlooks the lake with the symmetrical cone of the mountain beyond.

Silver Star Mountain (4390') is north of the Columbia River and south of Mt. St. Helens. Drive east from Battleground on Road N420 along East Fork Lewis River to Sunset Campground. Turn right on Road N412 which follows Copper Creek about 2 ½ miles, crosses it west and continues to the summit of Silver Star. Snow usually closes the road 3 miles or so from the top. The view is of Adams and Hood on either side of the Columbia Gorge and St. Helens to the north; an evening trip with the city lights below is spectacular.

Mt. Adams

Mt. Adams (12,326') is the legendary north guardian of the Columbia River. The south-side route has the fewest technical climbing problems for a winter ascent, compared to the other volcanic peaks in Washington. The gradient is gentle, and the route crosses no glaciers; distance, elevation, cold and snow conditions are the factors affecting a winter summit climb. This mountain probably enjoys more sunny days in winter than any other in the Washington Cascades. Early winter attempts are best as one can often drive to Wicky Creek Shelter (3350') in late December, although in winters of heavy snow the road is closed about 1 mile north of Trout Lake.

Trout Lake (register here with the U.S. Forest Service) is reached via State 121 from White Salmon on the Columbia River. Follow N80 from Trout Lake, then N81. Besides Wicky Creek, with its pot-bellied stove, there are shelters 3 miles beyond at Morrison, and 2 ½ miles farther at Cold Spring (5500').

Cold Spring or Timberline (about 5500') are a little low for high camp, but a party in good condition can make the summit climb and return, even on short days, by a pre-dawn start. Snow is usually wind-packed and firm above 6500 feet.

Scramble around left base of South Butte and up slopes beyond which gentle out at Lunch Counter area (9000' to 9500') where snowshoes and skis can usually be left. This is a poor high camp; some parties have been caught several days by storm in this exposed location. Slopes above steepen and crampons are used to the false summit at 11,700 feet, and the last 600 feet to the frigid summit. Usually the long slope below the false summit is wind-blasted and firm, although small areas of near-windslab are common.

The nearest peaks are so distant that the summit view is rather detached: on a clear day one can see from Mt. Baker near the Canadian border to Hood, Jefferson, and the Three Sisters in Oregon.

Arctic gear similar to that required on Rainier is a must. As on all above-timberline areas, care must be used to mark the return trail. In white-out conditions there are no landmarks to guide one down the featureless open slopes at the base of this mountain.

DESTINATION	Elevation: Highest or Starting (+)	Elevation Gain	Miles: Round Trip or One Way (*)	Time	Map on Page
Hogback Mtn. (from chairlift)	6,789	825	5	4-5 hours	12
Shoe Lake (from chairlift)	6,600	1,500 to lake 800 return	8	2 days	12
Sand Lake	5,295	900	7	6-8 hours or 2 days	12
Mt. St. Helens	9,677	5,277	5	8-10 hours	14
Abraham Flat	4,850	400 to pass 400 return	4	6-8 hours	14
Coldwater Peak	5,727	2,527	11	8-10 hours	14
Bear Pass	4,905	1,705	8-9	8-10 hours	14
Silver Star Mtn.	4,390	2,800	5	5-7 hours	15
Mt. Adams (from Wicky Creek)	12,326	9,000	22	3-4 days	16

MAPS

Topographic
White Pass   (15-minute)
Spirit Lake   (15-minute)
Mt. St. Helens   (15-minute)
Mt. Adams   (15-minute)

U.S. Forest Service
Mt. St. Helens - Spirit Lake Recreation Guide
Gifford Pinchot National Forest
 (Ranger District maps as available)

Chapter 2

MT. RAINIER NATIONAL PARK

Mt. Rainier is the most familiar mountain landmark in the Washington Cascades. Its 14,410-foot elevation is high enough to retain snow for some type of skiing almost all year, although a long carry may be required to ski summer runs such as that below 10,000-foot Camp Muir. Snow for ski touring and snowshoeing is often available from late October until May.

Avalanche hazard is high during and after snowstorms, although the open areas above timberline are so constantly wind-blasted and exposed to the sun that they firm up much faster than the wooded ridges and small peaks below 8000 feet. The greatest avalanche hazard to snow travelers is probably in this lower area, where more warming tends to release avalanches. The mountain has been climbed from all sides in winter conditions. Much more popular, however, are the areas of lower, smaller summits and ridges of 5000 to 8000 feet elevation, which are more accessible and better suited to day hikes by the average snowshoer or ski tourer.

Forests on lush valley floors are magnificent, ranging from cedar to hemlock, Douglas and other firs as well as some yew trees. Deciduous species range from alder to maple to cottonwood; whitebark pine and alpine fir are the common timberline species. Tree size decreases with increased elevation.

There are special rules concerning winter cross-country and back-country travel and camping in the Park. Mainly these involve registering at the nearest trail head or ranger station for hiking, or more detailed sign-out for summit climbs and reservations to stay at Camp Muir and Camp Schurman. Access to the Park is by the roads to the three entrance stations.

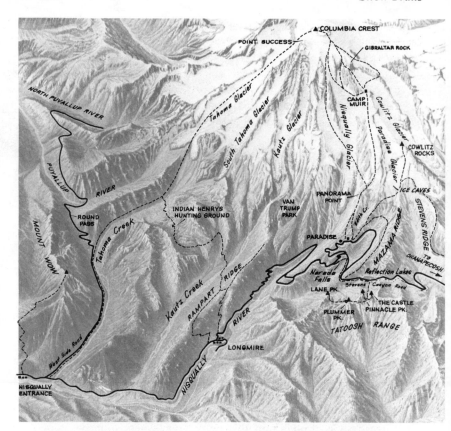

From copyrighted full-color map of Mount Rainier, courtesy of Dee Molenaar.

Nisqually Entrance

Nisqually entrance (2003') is reached via State 7 east through Ashford. **Mt. Wow** (6030') is north of Nisqually entrance. Locate the old trail, or follow Park boundary markers north of the road, to the crest of a ridge at 4000 feet, about 2 miles. Follow this minor ridge east to where it joins the main ridge, continuing north to the summit in about ½ mile. No doubt the view of Rainier explains the name of the peak.

About 1 mile inside the Park, **West Side Road** forks north off the road to Longmire. An excellent, gentle route for touring and hiking with occasional views of Rainier above, it is open to snowmobiles. A special viewpoint is at Round Pass, 7 miles. Shorter tours for beginners can be equally rewarding, with time spent exploring off the road and close beside Tahoma Creek.

Rampart Ridge trail makes a loop with excellent views of the south side of Rainier. It begins at Longmire and switchbacks out of Nisqually

Canyon west through heavy forest to the 4000-foot ridge crest. Deep snow may obscure the trail as it follows the ridgetop north about a mile, then descends slightly to a junction where the trail to Indian Henry's Hunting Ground forks left and the Van Trump Park trail continues on up the ridge. Return to Longmire on the right fork; 4.7 miles.

Indian Henry's Hunting Ground (5200') can be reached in 4.8 miles from the Rampart Ridge trail junction. A shorter approach is by Tahoma Creek trail, 3.6 miles from West Side Road, provided the road is free of snow. Crossing Tahoma Creek may be a problem as the suspension bridge is removed early in winter to prevent damage to the structure by excessive snow load. The view of Rainier is excellent, and the shelter cabin luxurious compared to a tent or the dank chill of the stone shelter at Muir. Touring the meadows on a cold, clear winter day is especially rewarding.

A large, gentle area for hiking and touring surrounds **Reflection Lakes** (4861'). Peaks of the Tatoosh Range challenge the climber. Park at Narada Falls, climb over the roadside snowbank and follow the stream, or climb the opposite hillside to Stevens Canyon Road above. The open slope to the right avalanches at times. Follow the road south, then east, to the lakes, which are flatter sections of what appears to be a large, rolling plain. The area is popular for overnight camping, with plenty of forest for shelter from wind. The views north of Rainier and the Tatoosh Range south are unobstructed.

One can wander among the lakes, hike or tour high up **Mazama Ridge,** which leads up the slope above the lakes. A loop can be made by continuing up the ridge, traversing west to Paradise, and back to the parking area at Narada.

A longer ski tour follows Stevens Canyon Road to Ohanapecosh on Highway 123, 23 miles north of State 12. Snow conditions must be stable as the section from Reflection Lakes to Box Canyon on the Cowlitz, at 10 miles, avalanches heavily; in places the road grade is filled completely. It is 12.7 miles from Box Canyon to Highway 123. This can be done in a long day by a strong party in good condition.

Four peaks of the Tatoosh Range are easily ascended if snow is stable. Steep slopes avalanche frequently onto the route leading to the pass between **Castle Peak** (6500') on the east and **Pinnacle Peak** (6562') to the west, as well as on the open upper slopes of these mountains. From the pass swing west onto the south side of Pinnacle and continue to the top; usually some icy rock scrambling near the top.

Castle Peak is most easily climbed by traversing east from the pass, then angling up to the exposed summit over steep, often icy and snow-covered rock pitches. **Plummer Peak** (6300') is southwest of Pinnacle.

Traverse to the pass between these two peaks and ascend south up gentle slopes to the summit. **Lane Peak** (6000') is west of Pinnacle. From the pass between Pinnacle and Plummer, traverse west past the basin containing Cliff Lake and continue northwest to the summit. The view of Rainier is outstanding; St. Helens and Adams loom in the south.

Paradise (5400') is a very heavily used winter sports center. Some tourists do not even get out of their cars, although it may be impossible to see Rainier over the roadside snowbanks, while others go no farther than the visitor center with its museum and snack bar. Nearby slopes attract those who enjoy sliding on inner tubes. Rope tows are popular with the downhill skiers, who rely on developed activity on the 30-40 acres occupied by such facilities.

Beyond these concentrated recreational opportunities extend miles of lovely snow-covered winter wilderness which attracts snowshoers, ski tourers and a large group of downhill skiers who tour to high areas to find untracked runs. Paradise is ideal for beginners and experts alike, provided they do not become confused in the frequent white-outs. When clouds or storm move in and white snow on the ground merges with white, blowing snow clouds, all landmarks are blotted out and it is difficult or impossible to distinguish up from down.

The **base of Panorama Point** (6300') is a good beginners' hike or tour. The view is of the peak above, and St. Helens and Adams beyond the Tatoosh peaks. Bypass the ski area on the west and continue north among the groves of trees, first in one minor stream gully, then another, more or less on the ridge above Nisqually Glacier. The snow ridge at about 6300 feet just below the steep 400-500-foot face of Panorama is a good turnaround point. The face is wind-blasted by storms from the southwest and is usually regarded as safe from avalanches. Records indicate, however, that it slides quite frequently, and a growing number of persons have received a free ride down it. A rule of thumb is offered: if the snow is soft enough to snowshoe up, there may be avalanche hazard; if the slope is so hard that snowshoes are better removed for stepkicking, there is less chance of it sliding. The view from the top of Panorama is just a little better than from the base, but the steep section is quite strenuous.

Paradise Ice Caves (6200') are popular in summer and winter. Follow the summer trail route as it angles east from the trail to Panorama Point, traversing across the head of Edith Creek to the cave beneath the terminus of Paradise Glacier. This can be strenuous, but with good, firm snow conditions is not difficult. As with all winter routes above timberline on broad, featureless snowfields, beginners, as well as experts, have routefinding problems when a storm suddenly moves in and creates white-out conditions. One party which became lost on return from the caves experienced a fatality.

A possible extension of a tour to Paradise Ice Caves leads to Cowlitz Rocks (7457') above Cowlitz Glacier. The long traverse across Paradise Glacier is usually smooth and gentle. Ski touring is often excellent on Stevens Ridge southeast of the caves. Continue on this route as far as time and energy permit, allowing enough of both to return to Paradise.

A more strenuous route leads to **Camp Muir,** which at 10,000 feet elevation, directly below Gibraltar Rock, is higher than most summits in the Cascades. On a clear, sunny warm spring day it is a long, gentle walk with a really outstanding view. For skiers it is also a great downhill run to Paradise. In mid-winter with deep, fresh snow it may be an impossible objective, or require several days. It is desirable to mark the route with wands, as clouds frequently move in and make routefinding on the descent difficult. Although the stone shelter at Muir is open to the public on a reservation basis, winter as well as summer, there are certain advantages in carrying a tent. Some parties have not had the strength to get to Muir in one day, and obviously a bivouac on these open snowfields in a storm is a serious proposition, and at best an unpleasant way to spend a long winter night.

Climbing parties have ascended **Rainier** by several routes from Camp Muir, or nearby, in winter. Glacier travel can be simpler in winter, as most crevasses are solidly bridged and routefinding is more direct, with fewer detours around crevasses. However, not all bridged crevasses are filled to the bottom with snow. Blowing snow often builds a cornice out from one edge of the crevasse until it reaches the other lip, and in the process a great deal of snow falls into the crevasse. Each new storm adds depth to the crevasse thus bridged and soon the strength of the bridging snow is considerable. Early winter, of course, will find weaker bridging than after several heavy snowfalls have occurred. Avalanching snow fills many crevasses. But one never knows for sure the strength of the bridges, or for that matter just where they are; ropes **must** be used for winter glacier touring. Testing bridges with the ax or ski pole is useless, as fresh snow is soft and offers no resistance. However, snowshoes or skis increase the supporting surface and there is less danger of poking a foot through a weak bridge while thus shod. A crevasse rescue with snowshoes or skis is awkward, as it is difficult to remove these devices while dangling from the end of a rope, or to put the snowshoe or ski into the stirrup or sling. It is best to leave snowshoes or skis attached to boots, and put the boot heel, rather than the toe, into the sling.

If camp is to be in an exposed position high on the mountain, only an expedition quality tent can take the stress of the high winds. Even in summer, tents used at Muir and Steamboat Prow have been damaged by the erratic gusts, and winter storms sometimes last several days. Arctic clothing, including heavy down or insulated jacket, extra warm insulated mitts, double boots and/or insulated gaiters and face mask, added to "standard" winter climbing gear, will give adequate protection to the body when it is -5°F on the summit with a 20-mile-per-hour wind (conditions can be much more severe than this).

The problem of short days can be minimized with an early start and a good flashlight. However, winter outdoorsmen, whether climbing to the top of Mt. Rainier or hiking meadows beside the highway, should maintain better physical condition than would be considered necessary in summer. The load is heavier, weather is more severe, and the penalty for mistakes higher; it is necessary to prepare more carefully for these strenuous winter trips. Snowfall patterns are different every year; check on conditions and prepare for whatever the snow or weather may be. Parties have been pinned down at Muir for several days by storm because they hadn't marked the return trail well enough and were afraid of becoming lost on the descent. Some groups have waited out storms in the steam caves on the summit. While many parties attempt a winter ascent of Rainier, few actually succeed.

Routes climbed or descended in winter from this entrance include Ingraham Glacier, Gibraltar Ledge and Chutes, Nisqually Icefall, Fuhrer Finger, and Tahoma Glacier. Ingraham Glacier usually resembles a snowfield when the yawning crevasses are filled or bridged with snow; it is often used as a descent route if the ascent is a steeper climb, as on the west and north side routes.

Carbon River Entrance

State 165 leads from Buckley to Carbon River entrance (1716') at the northwest corner of Mt. Rainier National Park. The road is frequently free of snow to the Park boundary at this low elevation, for on the warm west side of the Cascades, winter precipitation often falls as rain rather than snow, and snow will usually soon melt off. Check on snow and road conditions before planning a trip here; early and later winter are best times for a visit.

Mowich Lake Road forks off Carbon River Road some distance before the Park entrance. The road is gated at Park boundary and closed in winter at 2800 feet. **Mowich Lake** (4929') is reached in about 5 miles from this point. A shortcut saving a mile or so is the summer trail route from about 4200 feet, leading east across the road switchbacks and directly toward the lake.

The hike up **Fay Peak** (6500') begins from the ranger station east of the lake, due east up a gully to Knapsack Pass (6000') (provided the snow is stable) and contours southwest to the ridge which leads to the summit. There is a slight bench on the west side of Fay Peak which provides a gentle route for skiers. Follow the bench south and ascend southwest ridge to the summit. The view of Ptarmigan Ridge is truly magnificent.

A longer tour from Knapsack Pass to Spray Park follows the ridge to Mt. Pleasant. Traverse the south side of Mt. Pleasant to avoid a steep cliff on the north above Cataract Creek. The 1 ½-mile Eunice Lake trail to Ipsut Pass to the north is a short tour from Mowich Lake. Both of these provide outstanding views of the mountain above.

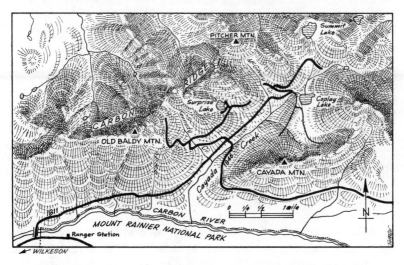

Old Baldy Mountain (5795') is located north of and outside the Park boundary on the northeast side of Carbon River; it has an excellent view of the north side of Rainier. Road 1811 forks north off Carbon River Road just outside the Park and crosses Carbon River. Follow it about 2 miles and take a left fork up Kennedy Creek. Ascend west to a ridgetop, follow it to about 4000 feet and angle left into a bowl. Climb northwest to the ridge above and follow it about ¼ mile east to the summit. **Coplay Lake,** another possible objective, is about 2 miles on Road 1811 east of Kennedy Creek.

Just inside the northwest corner of the Park is a group of peaks, actually high points on the ridge north of Eunice Lake. Do not let the moderate elevation of the summits suggest that these are better suited to Sunday afternoon strollers than winter mountaineers.

The starting elevation below 2000 feet determines a fairly long climb out of the valley. **Florence Peak** (5501') is reached via West Side Boundary trail starting at the entrance station. Follow the trail 2 ½ miles as it crosses a broad, forested ridge (4000'). Leave the trail, head east and continue as the ridge narrows to the summit in about ½ mile.

Two other peaks to the east are reached from Green Lake trail, which starts from the Carbon River Road about 3 ½ miles east of the entrance station. The winter route to **Arthur Peak** (5471') is mostly cross-country. Leave the trail at 2500 feet, before it enters the steep-sided canyon of Ranger Creek about ¾ mile from the road. Continue west up slopes above the trail, ascending to the north ridge of Arthur, which is followed south about 1 mile to the summit if snow is stable on steep slopes.

Gove Peak (5321') is the high point on the ridge east of Green Lake. Continue to Green Lake by trail, cross stream and climb east up the steep, forested slope beyond to the ridge leading southwest. A gentle area at 4200 feet slopes up to the steep narrow ridge to the summit in about ½ mile. If snow is unstable stay off steep slopes. The view of the north side of Rainier is most impressive from these peaks. The three great ridges — Curtis on the east, Liberty in the center, and Ptarmigan on the west — are somewhat obscured by distance, and Willis Wall assumes a rather sinister character. The frequent clouds of snow blowing off Liberty Cap, the 14,112-foot high point above, gives clear evidence that man must be a hurried visitor to the brutal summit environment in winter.

Winter ascents of Rainier from this side have been mostly unsuccessful. That the low elevation approach road is free of snow to feasible walking distance of the climbing routes is helpful, but from the road end at 2300 feet there is still 12,000 feet of elevation gain to **Liberty Cap,** then a descent to 13,500 feet and another 1000 feet of elevation gain to the summit. Also these routes are technically the most difficult on the mountain. The possibility of snow avalanches is always present and ice avalanches from the 300-foot high cliff of the summit ice cap occur all winter long. It is unusual to have enough days of good weather for the 4-5 days necessary for the climb and descent. The difficulty of retreat off these routes is such that only a few climbers commit themselves to a climb unless fairly certain of the weather.

Two advantages must be mentioned: the snow-covered Carbon Glacier is a veritable highway in the winter, when the crevasses are covered, and snowcover and cold temperatures eliminate rockfall on any of these routes. The West Rib of Willis Wall was ascended to the

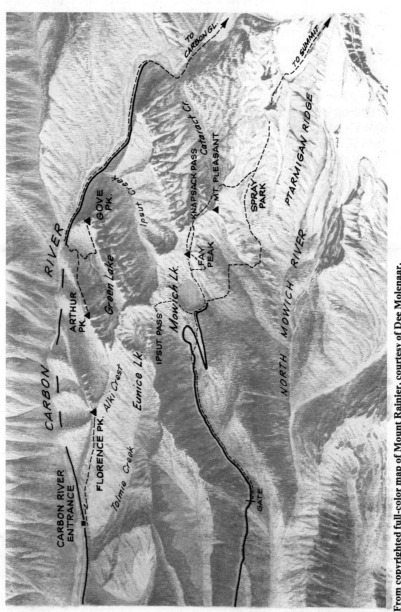

From copyrighted full-color map of Mount Rainier, courtesy of Dee Molenaar.

summit ice cliff in February, with a descent of Liberty Ridge. Liberty Ridge has been climbed several times in April and May, with descents of the ridge, or the Emmons Glacier to either White River entrance or return via Winthrop Glacier and back to the Carbon. Spring conditions are much more practical for these climbs.

Ptarmigan Ridge was climbed in early March, with the descent to Paradise. The party was caught by a storm in an exposed camp at 12,500 feet for two days, first in tents until these failed, then in quickly dug snow caves. The Central Rib of Willis Wall was climbed in May, and a winter-strength storm blew in during the ascent. The climb from the exit through the summit ice cliff to Liberty Cap was up steep slopes in chest-deep snow. The snow-cave bivouac at Liberty Cap was nearly a disaster, with wind-blown snow at first sealing the opening. Escape was at the cost of climbing rope and other gear. Four more days were necessary for the descent of the Emmons Glacier and hike out to the road, one truly necessary day being spent resting in the shelter at Camp Schurman. Three feet of new snow fell on Carbon Glacier during this storm, not in winter season, but in mid-May. The lure of routes such as these will no doubt lead to more attempts in the future. See **Cascade Alpine Guide** for details on climbing Mt. Rainier.

White River Entrance

The northeast corner of Rainier National Park is probably least used in winter as White River Road, formerly closed at the entrance station, is now closed several miles from the Park boundary. Access is via U.S. 410 east from Enumclaw. The highway is kept plowed just south of the turnoff to Crystal Mountain Ski Area at time of writing.

White River Road itself makes a good tour from the entrance station (3500') 7 miles to White River Campground (4400'). The grade is gentle with some climbing on the return. It is also open to snowmobile use.

A strenuous day tour to Sunrise Park is scenically rewarding, as the view of Rainier from that high point is excellent. Follow the trail from White River Campground about 2 ½ miles to the 6400-foot area above. A return via the road is easier as the grade is much gentler than the trail. A shortcut to bypass one road switchback to Sunrise Point descends the draw southeast to the next switchback below. Follow the road from here as the draw becomes very brushy and steep below. Approximately 24 miles round trip from White River entrance station.

Owyhigh Lakes (5150') may be reached by an avalanche-free route, 2 ½ miles by road to Shaw Creek trail and 3 miles to the lakes in their basin with high ridges above. There is a shelter cabin at the lakes.

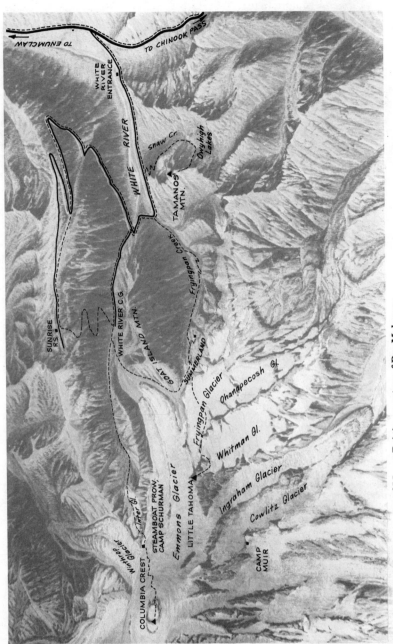

From copyrighted full-color map of Mount Rainier, courtesy of Dee Molenaar.

Tamanos Mountain (6850') is the high point on the avalanche-swept ridge west of the lakes. If the snow is stable, ascend steep slopes from lake to ridgetop, then north to the summit. The view of Emmons Glacier side of Rainier and Little Tahoma Peak is nearly as impressive as from Fay Peak farther west.

A winter visit to **Summerland** (5440') is also outstanding for scenery. This is a fairly long trip; an overnight stay is probably more practical than a one-day tour. Follow White River Road 3 ½ miles from entrance station to Fryingpan Creek, then take the trail 4 ¼ miles to the basin between the terminus of Fryingpan Glacier and Goat Island Mountain on the north. The shelter is at a grove of trees on a higher bench slightly to the east. Several major avalanche chutes deposit in the last forest before the snow-covered meadows of Summerland open out; stable snow is necessary for a visit here. There are gentle areas for touring west to the moraine beside Emmons Glacier, and a late winter trip might find good downhill runs off the slopes beside and on Fryingpan Glacier above.

Stable snow is essential for touring on the slopes leading to the summit of **Little Tahoma Peak** (11,117'). Ascend slopes south of the Summerland shelter to the 9000-foot notch in the ridge east of the summit. Cross to the south side, traverse west and ascend to the summit up steep snow slopes. The summit ridge may be too corniced and dangerous to climb the last hundred feet or so to the top. The winter view of Rainier is outstanding.

A circuit of Goat Island Mountain is a very long one-day tour. Follow the trail to Emmons Glacier moraine, 1 ½ miles from White River Campground. Cross White River on bridge and continue on Emmons Glacier southwest. Stay out on the glacier and away from slopes of Goat Island Mountain, which avalanche. Ascend to the pass south of Goat Island Mountain and Summerland to the east. Distance is approximately 20 miles round trip from White River entrance station.

Rainier has been climbed via Emmons Glacier in winter. Follow the trail from White River Campground to Glacier Basin and up Inter Glacier beyond to 9500-foot Camp Schurman at Steamboat Prow. At present this is an emergency shelter and not open to the public in winter. This route is technically easiest of any on Rainier, but the approach in winter is long, when compared with the two-day ascents from Paradise. Several avalanche chutes menace the trail between White River and Glacier Basin.

DESTINATION	Elevation: Highest or Starting (+)	Elevation Gain	Miles: Round Trip or One Way (*)	Time	Map on Page
Mt. Wow	6,030	4,000	5	6-8 hours	20
West Side Road	2,150+	optional	optional	optional	20
Rampart Ridge	4,000	1,200	4.7	5-8 hours	20
Indian Henry's Hunting Ground	5,200	2,550	13	2-3 days	20
Reflection Lakes	4,861	400	5	5-6 hours	20
Mazama Ridge	5,500	1,000	5	5-7 hours	20
Pinnacle, Castle Plummer, Lane Peaks	6,000- 6,500	1,500- 2,000	6-10	6-8 hours or 2 days	20
Base of Panorama Point	6,300	900	4½	5-7 hours	20
Paradise Ice Caves	6,200	800	6	5-7 hours	20
Camp Muir	10,000	4,600	10	8-10 hours or 2 days	20
Rainier (from Paradise)	14,410	9,000	12 (approx.)	2-4 days	20
Rainier (from start of Tahoma Creek Trail)	14,410	11,500	16	4-6 days	20
Mowich Lake	4,929	2,125	10	6-8 hours	27
Fay Peak	6,500	3,700	12-14	12 hours or 2 days	27
Old Baldy Mtn. (from Road 1811)	5,795	4,000	8	6-8 hours	25
Coplay Lake	3,865	2,025	8	6-8 hours	25
Florence Peak	5,501	3,800	6	6-8 hours	27
Arthur Peak	5,471	3,300	5	6-8 hours	27
Gove Peak	5,321	3,270	6	6-8 hours	27
Liberty Cap (from Ipsut Creek)	14,112	11,812	24 (approx.)	5-6 days	29
White River Road	3,500+	optional	optional	optional	30
Owyhigh Lakes (from White River entrance)	5,150	1,650	11	8-10 hours or 2 days	30
Tamanos Mtn. from White River entrance)	6,850	3,380	13	10-12 hours or 2 days	30
Summerland (from White River entrance)	5,440	1,970	16	2-3 days	30
Little Tahoma Peak (from White River entrance)	11,117	7,647	22 (approx.)	3-4 days	30
Rainier (from White River entrance)	14,410	10,900	30 (approx.)	6-7 days	30

MAPS

Topographic
Mt. Rainier   (15-minute)
Enumclaw   (15-minute)
Mt. Rainier   (7½-minute)

U.S. Forest Service
Mt. Baker - Snoqualmie National Forest
  (White River Ranger District)

Other
Mount Rainier National Park; pictorial relief map by Dee Molenaar

Chapter 3

U.S. 410—NORTH AND EAST OF MT. RAINIER

North and east of Mt. Rainier is an area of sharp, forested ridges and deep valleys, and a number of bare rocky summits. In summer the dominant impact is logging, cut through by a stream of tourists. When snow closes the back roads, however, solitude returns and, with the magnificent scenic backdrop of Rainier, changes this into a first-rate recreational area.

The heavy forest of fir, hemlock and cedar in valley bottoms has mostly been logged off, although some roadside stands of huge old trees remain. Logging clearcuts of 30 years ago are now masked by lush new trees. As elevation increases, tree height declines. Wind-blasted ridgetops support waist-high shrubs of alpine fir, whitebark pine and juniper. Some "mountains" have trees on their summits, but at Chinook Pass and Crystal Mountain, especially, summits are steep, rocky, bare of trees, and fraught with avalanche hazard.

At higher elevations such as Cayuse Pass snowfall is very heavy, nearly equal to that on Mt. Baker. At time of writing U.S. 410 is plowed east from Enumclaw to near Crystal Creek, south of Crystal Mountain Ski Area access road. For a brief era this route was kept plowed to Cayuse Pass, and State 123 beyond to the junction with State 12 over White Pass, thus providing winter recreationists easy access to both Chinook Pass area and White River entrance section of Mt. Rainier National Park. It is to be hoped that this practice can be resumed, because there are excellent winter routes in these places; they are included here, as snow travelers can walk the extra 4 miles to Cayuse Pass, and spend a night if necessary. However, early winter, before 410 is closed by snow, and late spring, after the snow has melted off, will be preferred times for trips here.

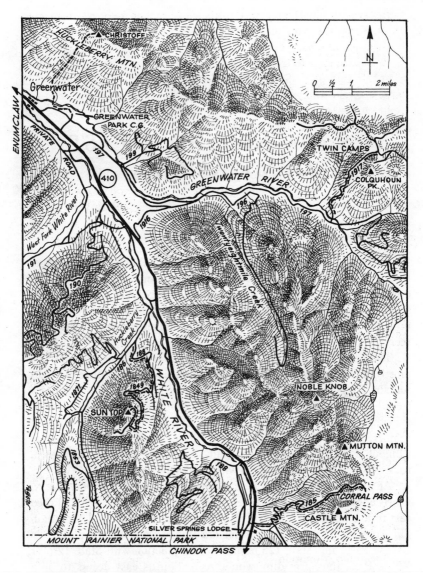

Huckleberry Mountain (4764'), northeast of the community of Greenwater, 17 miles east of Enumclaw on U.S. 410, is an excellent hike with a grand view of Mt. Rainier. The summit formerly was the site of Christoff Lookout. About 1 ¼ miles east of Greenwater fork east off 410 to Weyerhaeuser Timber Company's Greenwater Park Campground, about ¾ mile. If the access road is impassible due to snow or mud, arrange parking off the highway (parking on shoulders of State routes is prohibited), and walk to the campground beside Greenwater River. Cross the river on footbridge at Greenwater Park, or if it has washed out, at vehicle bridge ⅛ mile downstream. Return upstream on north side of river to trail signed Huckleberry Mountain trail, which is Christoff trail on U.S.G.S. map. Follow the trail northwest across a large clearcut where it has been obliterated. Locate it in timber to the right on far side; it leads to a minor ridge which rises northeast. At about 3500 feet the slope gentles and a clearing permits better views. Continue to the ridgetop above if snow is stable on open slopes. The summit is ¼ mile east.

West of U.S. 410 and north of Mt. Rainier National Park there are several logging roads which offer good touring and hiking routes. About 4 miles east of Greenwater fork west on **West Fork White River Road 191,** which extends about 15 miles to the Park boundary. Many roads lead off it in either direction to viewpoints east and west on Huckleberry Ridge (not the one near Greenwater).

Greenwater Road 197 in Greenwater Canyon offers hiking and touring routes although it is heavily used by snowmobiles. Turn east 2 miles east of Greenwater on Road 197, or 4 miles, where Road 1916 forks off 410 and quickly connects to Road 197. At times 197 may be snowcovered and good for touring. Quite often, however, it can be driven several miles and hikes started up side roads to viewpoints on ridges above.

Road 1917 forks north about 7 miles from 410 and leads to Twin Camps Campground (4169') in 3 miles. The road extends 3 miles east to Cascade Crest at Windy Gap (5200') with a view east to Mt. Stuart. At some switchbacks there are views of Chimney Rock peaks north of Snoqualmie Pass, and of Rainier. Other roads extend from Twin Camps toward Kelly Butte and Colquhoun Peak nearby. Beyond Twin Camps road other roads diverge off Road 197 up Twentyeight Mile Creek and toward Naches Pass at the head of Greenwater Canyon.

About 6 ½ miles from Greenwater, Huckleberry Creek Road 186 turns west off U.S. 410, crosses White River, and, with many spurs, continues south to Mt. Rainier National Park; many miles of gentle road. **Suntop Mountain** (5270') is an excellent objective with a closer view of Mt. Rainier and the minor peaks, ridges, and valley of this area. Leave Huckleberry Creek road on Road 188 and continue east to summit on Road 1849. A shortcut leaves the road north of the peak and follows the ridgetop south to the summit.

Corral Pass Road 185 forks east off U.S. 410 just north of Silver Springs Lodge, reaching the 5650-foot pass in 6 miles. There are good views of Rainier to the west along the way, and from open areas east of

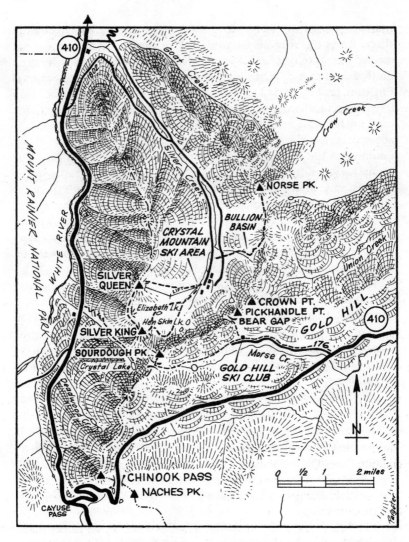

the pass, Mt. Stuart can be seen. Depending on time and energy, one can continue to a nearby 6333-foot point on Castle Mountain, with exceptional views of Rainier. To the north is more open ridgecrest inviting one to tour or hike to high points with whimsical names such as Mutton Mountain and Noble Knob.

Crystal Mountain Ski Area (4400') is 38 miles east of Enumclaw on U.S. 410, the last 6.3 miles on access road which turns east a little south of Silver Springs Lodge. The peaks on the ridges rimming the ski area in the south end of Silver Creek valley are frequent objectives of snow travelers. These, and the basins separating the peaks, are long-time favorites of alpine skiers. Morse Creek Canyon, just over the Cascade Crest to the south with its private Gold Hill Ski Club, is visited frequently by skiers from Crystal. Morse Creek skiers also cross the divide and enjoy the runs to the north.

For all routes arrange parking in ski area lots. Use designated overnight area if the trip is an overnight stay. Register with Ski Patrol in day lodge and check on snow and avalanche conditions, especially if not familiar with the terrain and weather.

Silver King Peak (7012'), on the west side of the valley, is the highest summit in the area and the high point on the ridge labelled Crystal Mountain on maps. The view west of nearby Mt. Rainier and Little Tahoma Peak is especially enticing from the top of the mountain. Follow Quicksilver Lift on west side; stay off all ski runs. At second exit for Queens Run head southwest up canyon to Elizabeth Lake (5800'). Ascend from here to notch in ridge to the south (6100'), and follow this ridge west to the summit. Campbell Basin above the lake is large and has good campsites.

An alternative route is to continue south past the upper terminal of Quicksilver Lift to Hen Skin Lake and Miners Lakes in Silver Basin. Angle west up forested slopes to the 6100-foot notch south of Elizabeth Lake and continue to the summit. If snow is unstable do not use routes on open slopes.

On that superb day when it is clear, snow is stable, and the party is strong and eager, continue north on the ridgecrest to Silver Queen Peak (7002'). There is a slight descent to Crystal Col and a short climb to the Throne (6600'), then another descent to Campbell Col and the last climb to Silver Queen, about 1 mile from Silver King. Descend the east ridge. Skiers frequent the entire area, so snowshoers should stay off the runs — their plunge-step depressions in the snow are not appreciated by paying patrons.

Ski tourers may prefer to ski the slopes of Silver Basin rather than climbing these peaks. Black Tusk Gap, and Bear Gap, just southwest of Pickhandle Point, are routes to Morse Creek valley to the south. Each has good runs, although after storms there is avalanche hazard. An occasional party may follow the Crest Trail south to Chinook Pass and return when snow conditions are good.

Bullion Basin, east of the ski area, attracts snow travelers. The ridgetop above and **Norse Peak** (6856') to the north provide scenic objectives for a longer trip to a higher point with a better view. From Crystal Mountain chapel head east beside the lift, and ascend beside stream from the basin. There is avalanche hazard off open slopes

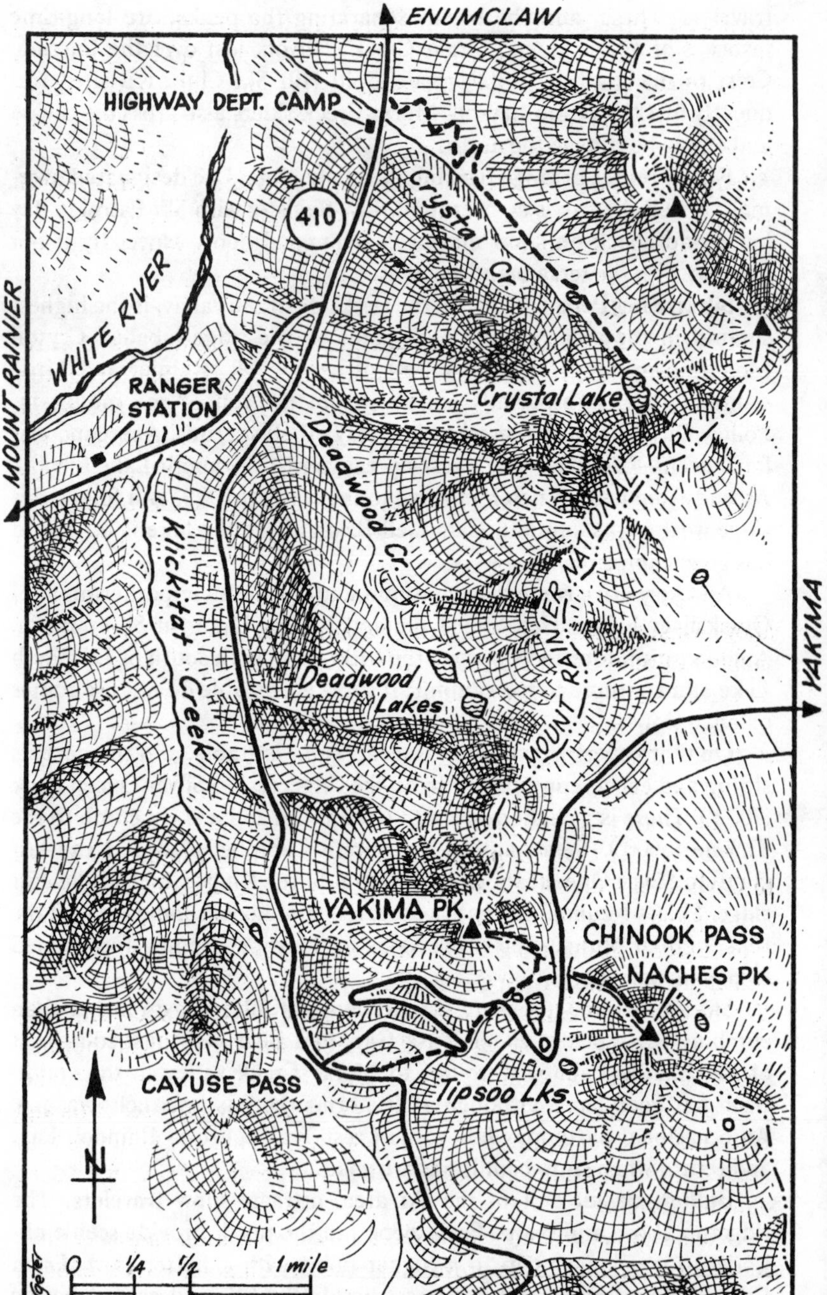
ENUMCLAW
HIGHWAY DEPT. CAMP
410
Crystal Cr.
WHITE RIVER
MOUNT RAINIER
RANGER STATION
Crystal Lake
MOUNT RAINIER NATIONAL PARK
Deadwood Cr.
Klickitat Creek
Deadwood Lakes
YAKIMA
YAKIMA PK.
CHINOOK PASS
NACHES PK.
CAYUSE PASS
Tipsoo Lks.
N
0
1/4
1/2
1 mile
Pargeter

northwest of the basin; the safest route is in forest on the south side of the stream. A level area at 5500 feet is a good turnaround for beginners.

Continue through timber up the last strenuous slope to the northeast until the ridgetop is reached. Open slopes frequently avalanche; avoid them. A nearby 6500-foot point offers a good view of Rainier, Adams, and peaks north and east. Norse Peak is about 1 ¼ miles north along the Cascade Crest. The ridge is often corniced on the east; stay well west of these fragile overhanging structures. Upon return from any route at Crystal Mountain Ski Area be sure to check out, or leave a note, with the Ski Patrol.

Crystal Lake (5830') lies in a steep walled cirque just south of Silver King Peak. Present winter road end on U.S. 410 and State Highway facility are just south of Crystal Creek (3600'), which drains this basin. Park at road end unless snow removal operations prevent. Follow trail route on north side of the stream through forest up this steep hillside about a mile to where the slope eases (about 4500'). The forest thins here and the steep, open slopes above avalanche into the basin from all sides; do not proceed on this route if snow is unstable.

The basin is lovely. There are good ski runs from the high ridges above when the snow is right, and pleasant hikes and scenery as well. A number of years ago, before U.S. 410 to Cayuse Pass was plowed, skiers used this route as access to Morse Creek, climbing through the 6400-foot pass north of Sourdough Peak and skied down into Morse Creek and Crystal Mountain Ski Area. Skiers have also climbed from the lake over the ridge and descended to the Crystal Mountain Ski Area. Both sides of the ridge are very steep.

Because the State Department of Highways has lengthened access to Cayuse Pass (4700') by about 4 miles by their decisions concerning plowing snow in winter, many routes must now be considered overnight trips. Skiers will have a definite advantage over snowshoers on the 4-mile downhill return from Cayuse Pass.

The route to **Chinook Pass** (5440') from Cayuse parallels Highway 123 south about ¾ mile past a slide area. Ascend in forest beyond, following the stream draining Tipsoo Lake, about 1 ½ miles to the lake. (The route followed by U.S. 410 crosses over and under sheer cliffs and is not practical for winter use, even on foot. Heavy snowfall in this area creates extreme avalanche hazard when temperatures rise after deep snow has fallen.)

The meadows around Tipsoo Lake are as lovely as in summer; there are sheltered campsites in groves of alpine fir. Chinook Pass is about a mile east and a few hundred feet higher than Tipsoo. Follow the highway route, if it can be seen, or wander more directly cross-country.

Snowmobiles are limited to U. S. 410 roadway in Chinook Pass-Lake Tipsoo area. **Yakima Peak** (6231') northwest of the pass, has been climbed in winter along the right of the ridge from the pass, then up a gully on the east side to the summit; snow must be stable for this climb. **Naches Peak** (6457') to the southeast has been approached via the ridge from the pass, but the last rope lengths are difficult on steep loose rock or ice. A more popular route is to a minor point (about 6000') on the ridge west of the summit, an excellent place to stop, eat lunch and enjoy the view of Rainier. The last section of ridge on this side requires rope and belay protection also.

Two areas reached from Yakima via U. S. 410 east of Chinook Pass are especially popular with skiers and snowshoers. Bumping Lake Road 174 turns south off U. S. 410 and is plowed to Goose Prairie (3265'). There are roads and gentle terrain here; the area is also quite popular with snowmobilers.

The 19-mile circuit of **Bumping Lake** (3426') is a good, strenuous trip, better for skis than snowshoes, as it is nearly level (high point 3600'). It is 2.4 miles from Goose Prairie to Bumping Lake Dam, 2.4 miles across the dam to end of Road 1602 on the north shore, 5 miles by trail south beyond the head of the lake, where there are campsites at

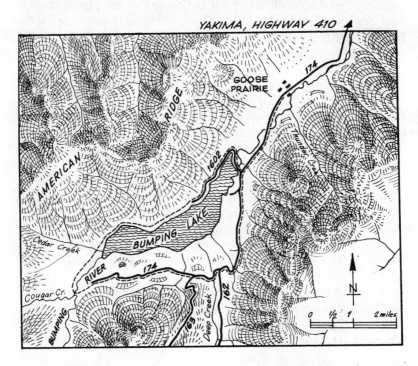

about the halfway point. Cross the river on a footlog or snowbridge, but be careful — it is a large stream. Road 174 is rejoined in ½ mile, and return to dam in 6.1 miles. On a clear day the top of Mt. Rainier may be seen, and the nearby peaks southeast of the lake are quite impressive when gleaming white with snow.

Morse Creek valley, already mentioned as accessible from across the Cascade Crest and Crystal Mountain Ski Area, has a long history of skiing. The hospitable Gold Hill Ski Club attracts both skiers and snowshoers to its cabin. Winter road end of U. S. 410 is about 9 miles east of Chinook Pass where Morse Creek is bridged by the highway. The 2-mile approach to the cabin from the highway, and nearby peaks for climbing and slopes for skiing make day trips to the area possible and attractive for local snow travelers.

Several short routes ascend to passes and peaks of the Cascade Divide just north of the valley. Gold Hill, directly behind the cabin, has

Touring at Ingalls Lake.

excellent skiing when snow is stable. Pickhandle Point (6240') and Crown Point (6500') to the north are scenic vantage points above Gold Hill. Bear Gap just west of Pickhandle provides access to Crystal Mountain side of the ridge. **Sourdough Peak** (6796') is 1 ½ miles west of Bear Gap and is easily ascended from Sourdough Pass, the low gap at valley head which is the summer route of the Cascade Crest Trail. The view of Rainier and Adams to the south is excellent. Heavy snowfall creates extreme avalanche hazard on all open slopes, especially during and after storms; good judgement is required to safely travel the routes beyond the cabin.

DESTINATION	Elevation: Highest or Starting (+)	Elevation Gain	Miles: Round Trip or One Way (*)	Time	Map on Page
Huckleberry Mtn. (from Greenwater River)	4,764	3,000	6	6-8 hours	34
West Fork White River Road 191	2,000+	optional	optional	optional	34
Suntop Mtn.	5,270	3,120	8	8-10 hours	34
Corral Pass	5,650	2,800	13	8-10 hours	34
Crystal Mtn. Ski Area	4,400+	optional	optional	optional	36
Silver King Peak	7,012	2,612	5	6-8 hours	36
Bullion Basin	5,500	1,100	3-4	5-6 hours	36
Norse Peak	6,856	2,456	10	8-10 hours	36
Crystal Lake	5,830	2,230	5	5-6 hours	38
Chinook Pass (from Crystal Creek)	5,440	2,000	13	8-10 hours	38
Yakima Peak	6,231	2,831	17	10-12 hours or 2 days	38
Naches Peak	6,457	3,057	17	10-12 hours or 2 days	38
Bumping Lake	3,600	335	19	2-3 days	40
Morse Creek Valley	4,500-5,000	500-1,000	4-5	4-5 hours	36
Sourdough Peak	6,796	2,800	10	8-10 hours	36

MAPS

Topographic
Greenwater	(15-minute)
Bumping Lake	(15-minute)
Lester	(15-minute)
Mt. Rainier National Park	(15-minute)

U.S. Forest Service
Mt. Baker - Snoqualmie National Forest
  (White River Ranger District)

Other
Crystal Mtn. Ski Area
Mount Rainier National Park; pictorial relief map by Dee Molenaar

Chapter 4

NORTH BEND TO SNOQUALMIE PASS

The geographic transition from lowland forest near Puget Sound to the high ridges and deep valleys of the west slope of the Cascades reflects in weather conditions. The west slope foothills force clouds dripping with Pacific Ocean moisture up where colder temperatures cause it to fall as snow rather than rain. Snow travelers often carry snowshoes and skis some distance up low-elevation valleys until they reach enough snow to need them. Frequently there is no snow along the roadside of Interstate 90 until 17.5 miles east of North Bend where the elevation at Asahel Curtis Forest Camp is 2000 feet, although there may be snow a short distance up side valleys.

Snow of depth adequate for snowshoeing or ski touring at lower elevations can have contradictory effects on the winter recreationist: Puget Sound area snowshoers and touring skiers will not have to drive far to start hiking, but snow plowed off roadways and left in high banks on either side limits parking so that lowland routes close to home are difficult to use. Parking is usually available to the resourceful, although cross-Cascade routes will present serious parking problems in winters of deep snow.

Temperatures near or above freezing results in sticky, heavy snow in the west slope areas. Cold, dry powder will be at a premium, and usually found only at higher elevations and on windy ridgetops. Forest cover is heavy, but a great deal of low unpleasant summer brush will be covered.

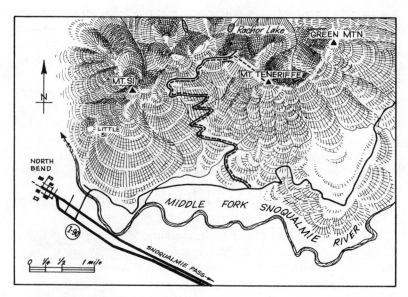

Mt. Teneriffe (4788') is the high point east of Mt. Si, the prominent peak towering over North Bend. From Mt. Teneriffe an outstanding panorama includes the Puget Sound area below, the Olympics beyond and Baker to the north, Rainier to the south and Snoqualmie peaks east. Beginners on skis or snowshoes probably will not ascend to the top, but there is good touring on roads on or near the valley floor.

Turn left off I-90 1 ½ miles east of North Bend on Mt. Si Road 2406 and proceed 5 miles to an unidentified but obvious gated logging road on the left (about 960'). Take the uphill (right) fork in 1 ½ miles. A 4-mile hike on this road leads to the ridgetop between Mt. Si on the left and Teneriffe ¾ mile to the right. Skis or snowshoes may be carried part way, depending on the time of year and snowfall. Road 2406 beyond this point offers touring, and there are other side roads and gentle terrain along the Middle Fork Snoqualmie River.

Logging roads branch off I-90 at various places between North Bend and Snoqualmie Pass; good touring for beginners. At former site of Camp Mason community, 11½ miles east of North Bend, there is a turnoff with a bridge across the South Fork Snoqualmie River close under the steep north side of McClellan's Butte. Peaks and valleys on both sides of the highway offer miles of touring as well as challenging ascents and excellent scenery.

The areas around **Mt. Kent** (5087') and **McClellan's Butte** (5162') are approached by following Tinkham Road 222 across the bridge. Take Road 2351 where it diverges and continue to its farthest loop up

Alice Creek. Leave the road and continue through forest along Alice Creek. Do not use the trail to McClellan's Butte, as it crosses several avalanche chutes. Several slide paths from Kent to the south and McClellan's Butte to the west menace this route; be sure snow is stable when crossing these open areas.

Lower Alice Lake (4400') is about 3 miles from I-90. Kent's summit is ¼ mile east, reached by a ridge from the lake. Turn right at the lake and proceed west toward McClellan's Butte for a change of scene. The ridge connecting it to Kent has a few ups and downs, and a good turnaround spot short of McClellan's airy summit, which is rarely climbed in winter. The view is good of the Snoqualmie Pass peaks, Rainier south and Puget Sound and the Olympics west.

Gentle valley floor and logging roads along the South Fork Snoqualmie River offer miles of touring and hiking for beginners.

Northeast of Camp Mason rises **Bandera Mountain** (5240'). At present almost all timber has been burned off this mountain's south side and it is even more hazardous for slides now than in 1956, when the author and a companion were injured there in an avalanche. A safer route, but one with plenty of slide potential, climbs to the summit via the west ridge. Park at Camp Mason and cross over I-90 at Mason Creek bridge if there is no room on the north side of the highway. Climb timbered slopes to Road 2218 which crosses Mason Creek, switchbacks across the stream again, and ends at about 2500 feet. If the snow is stable, continue east up steep slopes to the ridge and follow it to about 4500 feet where the ridge gentles. One hump has a 150-foot descent beyond, with the summit about 1 ½ miles from the 4500-foot elevation.

Bandera is separated from two peaks to the north by a high valley containing Mason, Little Mason, Kulla Kulla, Rainbow, Blazer, and Island Lakes. Beyond this 4500-foot high area rise Mt. Defiance, northwest of Bandera, and Pratt Mountain, to the northeast.

Mt. Defiance (5584') is most easily reached from the logging road approach for Bandera by continuing up Mason Creek. Steep, wooded slopes slightly west of the summit offer a route, or continue up Mason Creek, take the left (north) fork to Little Mason Lake (4250') and follow the southeast ridge just beyond the lake, which is the trail route, to the summit. To the east and north is the west side of the Snoqualmie peaks, with Rainier to the south and the Olympics to the west. There are steep open slopes on this route; check for unstable snow.

Pratt Mountain (5099') can be more easily reached by skirting the east side of Bandera, starting from near Bandera Airstrip. Park on Road 2218 beside I-90 and follow the right fork of Road 2218 to its end and continue ascending past the east ridge of Bandera to Talapus Lake

(3250'), about 2 miles. The creek beyond the lake is in a box canyon with steep, wooded walls with some danger of slides if the snow is unstable; avalanches flow through stands of trees without any one clearcut chute. Island Lake (4300') is in the high valley between Bandera and Pratt. Climb out of valley on north and avoid open slopes on the final ascent to the summit to the northeast.

Granite Mountain (5629') is due east, and the many peaks of the Snoqualmie group extend north and east. The nearby lakes below form a charming foreground for Bandera beyond and Rainier on the southern horizon. Park at Denny Creek Road or a turnout ½ mile west, beside the westbound lane of I-90, for the usual approach to Granite Mountain or touring on Denny Creek Road beside the river on the canyon bottom. The rather involved route circles west to avoid the open, avalanche-prone south slopes directly above the Denny Creek exit. Follow Pratt Lake trail 4 ½ miles to Olallie Lake shelter. The forest of huge cedars and firs obscures the view until an opening at 3 miles, and Olallie beyond. Head straight east from Olallie; as forest opens, aim for a pass between two 5000+-foot high points above. The slope is moderately steep; any danger of avalanche should dictate a retreat. From the pass continue on the south side of the north — left hand — high point and follow the ridgetop ½ mile or so east to the fire lookout on the summit. Crampons and ice ax may be desirable if the snow is frozen hard on the ridgetop.

The upper slopes provide good views of the Snoqualmie peaks, especially Kaleetan across frozen Tuscohatchie Lake to the north. The valley floor below presents what must be one of the worst examples available of too many roadways in a constricted mountain valley. Included are a trans-continental railway, a generous powerline swath with an unimproved road, the separated six-lane route of I-90, plus logging roads and interchanges. It has to be seen to be believed.

Beginners can reap a fringe benefit from the snowcovered roads, however, by ski touring or hiking them on snowshoes. The powerline swath is a little rough and has creeks and open water which cut off access along it. The railroad has a greater hazard when snow is deep, as it will be plowed to at least a 4-foot trench which can be a little tricky to scramble into and out of. Downhill locomotives come through fast and very quietly; post a lookout to give warning to beginners who may panic and get tangled up in their footgear when surprised by an oncoming train.

Humpback Creek, with its deep canyon leading south from I-90, is the obvious access route to a group of peaks south of the Snoqualmie River valley. Park on the south side of I-90, across from Asahel Curtis

Picnic Area, where there is often a plowed area, or drive or hike Humpback Creek Road to where the trail starts. Logging has disrupted the trail route; if it cannot be located, follow Humpback Creek on its east side, cross Milwaukee railroad in about ½ mile from I-90, and locate the trail, which stays 100 feet or more above the creek the entire route to **Annette Lake** (3650'), rising for the first 1 ½ miles in a series of switchbacks which may be difficult for inexperienced touring skiers. The lake, 2 miles beyond the switchbacks, is a good turnaround, camp spot or viewpoint with little avalanche hazard.

Silver Peak (5605'), to the east, can be climbed from the lake, provided the steep open slopes are not about to avalanche. At times they may be frozen hard and require ice axes, crampons, and rope. A 5000-foot pass south of Silver provides access to **Abiel Peak** (5365') south of the lake and **Tinkham Peak** (5395') about 1 ½ miles southeast of the lake. All three of these peaks have been climbed in one day by experienced parties in good condition.

A shorter way to Silver Peak takes a route which leaves the Humpback Creek trail about ¼ mile south of the railroad. Ascend the forested hillside directly east through heavy hemlock and fir forest on a fairly steep slope. In about ½ mile, at 3500 feet, the slope gentles; head south on the west edge of a rather flat area. The forest has more openings, allowing panoramic views. A small but definite valley drains the north side of Silver. Stay on the right (west) side of it and ascend to a knob or flat just north of the ridge leading to the summit. A steep scramble to a low point in the ridge west of the summit may be unstable, overhung by cornices, and quite dangerous. From ridgetop the summit is about 400 feet above. The view is spectacular, with the Snoqualmie peaks, notably Kaleetan, to the north and the broad swath of I-90 climbing from the west toward the summit. Lake Keechelus is to the east, with Stuart and Rainier, as always, dominating the eastern and southern horizons, and the Olympics to the west.

Olallie Meadows, the flat area north of Silver, can be reached by this route as well as from the summit or Hyak. Silver Peak can be ascended by the east ridge from the Meadows if snow is stable.

Humpback Mountain (5174') on the west side of Humpback Creek, has views as good as those of neighboring peaks, but the most noticeable feature of this ridge is the ridgetop-to-creek-bottom avalanche chutes. Follow Humpback Creek trail to the switchbacks which start at about 3000 feet elevation, 1 ½ miles from I-90. Cross creek and ascend steep forested areas to the ridgetop just south of the 4883-foot knob on the north end of the main ridge. The high point is south ¼ mile. This climb must not be attempted when there is any unstable snow.

DESTINATION	Elevation: Highest or Starting (+)	Elevation Gain	Miles: Round Trip or One Way (*)	Time	Map on Page
Mt. Teneriffe	4,788	3,800	12	10 hours	44
Mt. Kent	5,087	3,500	6	4-5 hours	53
McClellan's Butte	5,050	3,480	8	6-8 hours	53
Bandera Mtn.	5,240	3,668	8	6-8 hours	53
Mt. Defiance	5,584	4,012	10	8-10 hours	53
Pratt Mtn.	5,099	3,450	8	6-8 hours	53
Granite Mtn.	5,629	3,730	13	6-10 hours	53
Annette Lake	3,650	1,750	7	4-5 hours	53
Silver Peak	5,605	3,705	6	6-8 hours	53
Abiel Peak	5,365	3,465	9	6-8 hours	53
Tinkham Peak	5,395	3,500	10	6-8 hours	53
Humpback Mtn.	5,174	3,274	6	5-6 hours	53

MAPS

Topographic
Bandera	(15-minute)
Snoqualmie Pass	(15-minute)
Mt. Si	(15-minute)
North Bend	(15-minute)

U.S. Forest Service
Mt. Baker - Snoqualmie National Forest
  (North Bend Ranger District)

Other
The North Central Cascades; pictorial relief map by Richard A. Pargeter

Chapter 5

SNOQUALMIE PASS— SUMMIT AREA

Snoqualmie summit is probably the most popular snow travel area in Washington. The valleys and peaks rising from this 3000-foot gap through the Cascade Range have sufficient snow for skis or snowshoes from late December to late April or early May; then it becomes firm enough to walk on with climbing boots.

I-90 provides better access to Snoqualmie than is possible to any other area in the State. In the 50's and 60's there was roadside parking by the mile. At present, parking is restricted to small public areas on either side of Commonwealth Creek Bridge on Alpental Road and north of Hyak exit. If these are full, arrange for parking — sometimes for a fee — in one of the ski area lots. It is unfortunate that parking for use of the non-commercial public land has been sealed off by the State Highway Department for lack of funds. New legislation authorizes the sale of winter recreation parking permits with funds to be used for plowing and this will help correct the problem. Parking on the shoulders of State highways is not permitted except for emergencies, and those who park for recreation do so for a price — sometimes a fine and tow-away charge.

Once away from the car, the real charms of the area can be enjoyed. Those who prefer to stroll along the streams and wander through the forest can hike the gentle slopes on either side of the pass, on into Commonwealth Basin, or the valley beyond Alpental. Guye Peak and Chair

Peak seen from close beneath are impressive. However, climbing to open areas above the valley floor improves the views markedly. A little elevation gain will soon provide glimpses of Mt. Rainier to the south. Panoramas include — on that ideally clear day — the Olympics to the west, Stuart to the east, Glacier Peak to the north, and many nearby smaller peaks.

The predominantly fir and hemlock forest at the crest of the wet Cascades is lush and tall on valley floors but thins to battered sub-alpine conifer "bushes" on ridgetops and summits. Although it is possible to quickly approach very close to the peaks without risking avalanche danger greater than that involved in driving the highway itself, careful study of terrain is vital to safe snow travel in this area; most gullies in the high Cascades are so regularly swept by avalanches that no trees grow in them.

Low elevations and the influence of warm, wet air from the Pacific Ocean combine in winter to create considerable snow depth. Temperatures are moderate and powder snow unusual. Clothing and ski waxes must be suitable for moist conditions, although ridgetops consistently have sub-freezing temperatures and wind, and occasionally there are spells of near-zero weather.

Commonwealth Basin is a short, attractive hike for the novice skier or snowshoer. The route passes through deep forest of fir and hemlock and approaches steep peaks, yet is out of range of avalanches. If possible, park on Alpental Road ¼ mile from turnoff from I-90, where there is public as well as private parking. Two approaches lead to the basin 500 feet above, one on either side of Commonwealth Creek.

The route east of Commonwealth Creek follows the Cascade Crest Trail through heavy timber, then across a clearcut with views south to the ski areas of Snoqualmie Pass, and back into forest to a crossing of the cascading creek. The crossing may be difficult when deep snow creates vertical banks rising high above the footlog.

The route west of the creek involves skirting around — not across — the Sahale Ski Hill to the ridge above. Follow the ridge crest ¼ mile toward Guye Peak with occasional views past Alpental toward Chair Peak. Leave the ridge below the base of Guye Peak and make a gently climbing traverse to the right. The east and west routes join slightly below 3500 feet where the gradient eases.

The basin, or valley, extends about ½ mile farther, opening out wider with several forks of the creek draining the slopes of the four peaks — Guye, Lundin, Red, and Kendall — which rim the basin. At about 4000 feet the basin rises abruptly to these points above. Numerous gullies and open slopes feed avalanches into the basin, so be wary of blundering from gentle forest to open meadows which may be slide accumulation sites in winter. Wandering the basin floor among small ridges and the several creeks calls for a certain amount of enjoyable routefinding.

The peaks above Commonwealth Basin provide a much better view as well as demanding more snowshoeing and skiing skill. A winter ascent of **Guye Peak** (5168'), the lowest of the Snoqualmie Pass group, requires some mountaineering skill. Rising directly north of the pass and a familiar view to generations of skiers, this rocky spire presents its most impressive side to the highway; the winter route is on the gentler north side, reached from Commonwealth Basin. Enter Commonwealth Basin as just described. At about 3500 feet, however, swing left along the base of Guye, with one fork of the creek on the right. Cross this stream soon — it leads directly under avalanche gullies on the east and north sides of Guye. Gain the minor ridgetop just above the stream (northeast). Follow through heavy growth of trees to its end at 4000 feet. A small notch just before its abrupt end gives access to a small open flat below on the left (south). Cross the flat and angle steeply up to the left (south) to the upper creek valley which levels out beyond the traverse. A steep gully leads directly to Cave Ridge, which connects Guye Peak to Mt. Snoqualmie, but à route to the right of the gully through short, dense forest has less avalanche danger.

Avalanche control work at Alpental involves shooting Cave Ridge with artillery. **Check with the snow ranger at Snoqualmie Pass or Alpental before snowshoeing or skiing to Cave Ridge.** Avalanche control takes precedence over recreation here.

Traverse left (south) from this 4600-foot low point in the ridge to a level overlook of Alpental and the other ski areas. Distorted bits of music drift up as on one's view extends beyond Chair Peak, Denny Mountain, and Silver Peak to Mt. Rainier on the skyline. The slopes above the overlook lead to the north ridge and to the summit, and present the greatest avalanche hazard on the route. Follow the ridge, leaving snowshoes when snow becomes steep and hard. Traverse right (west) of the first rocky spire, which may call for roping up and belaying across the exposed slope to the notch beyond. A belay must be set to climb down the face of a snow-covered gendarme beyond the notch, and return. The summit rises just beyond. Care must be exercised on the ridgetop cornices, some of which overhang west and some east. During spells of warm weather in winters of light snowfall other routes may be climbed, but in true winter conditions even the north ridge may be too unstable to attempt.

The summit climb is practical for experienced climbers only and when there is no avalanche hazard. Stopping places short of the summit are the flat at 4000 feet, the gentle draw just below Cave Ridge, and Cave Ridge and overlook, which has a fair view and good places to camp. Probably skiers need more skill to comfortably descend the slopes below Cave Ridge than do snowshoers; beginning skiers especially should anticipate descending problems before climbing too high on steep wooded slopes.

Beyond Guye looms the rounded dome of **Mt. Snoqualmie** (6278'). Snowshoes and skis may be used to the summit, although several avalanche injuries have occurred on the open lower slopes of this peak. Avalanche control work on Cave Ridge affects this route; **check with snow ranger at Snoqualmie Pass or Alpental before starting up Mt. Snoqualmie.**

Approach as for Guye Peak. At about 4800 feet the rounded top of Cave Ridge, with several depressions in the snow indicating cave entrances, descends 50 feet to a level area. The lee slope above, leading to the south ridge of Snoqualmie, is the most critical. If it seems unstable, turn back and enjoy the views. Continue to the ridgetop beyond only if the snow is firm. The slopes on the opposite side of the ridge are also targets for artillery projectiles used in avalanche control.

The windswept ridgetop may be bare in places. The summit gives an excellent view of the local scene as well as the distant peaks. Early or late winter, and prolonged spells of good weather are best and safest for the ascent.

Lundin Peak (6057'), northeast of Snoqualmie, is not recommended for winter ascents. The approach from Commonwealth Basin leads into a gully system with unacceptably high avalanche hazard. **Red Mountain** (5890'), the pyramidal peak at the head of the basin, also has high avalanche hazard but can be a feasible objective. Continue to the head of Commonwealth Basin instead of swinging left around the base of Guye Peak. At 4000 feet the slopes steepen; follow the side draw out of Lundin Chute to the right, to the small flat at 4800 feet which is Red Pond beside the Cascade Crest Trail in summer. Any doubt about the stability of slopes above dictates a retreat. If conditions permit the ascent, ice axes and climbing gear are essential. The summit view is the best in the group, with Lemah Mountain, Chimney Rock and Overcoat Peak rising out of Burnt Boot Creek to the north, and nearer peaks, such as Mt. Thompson.

Kendall Peak (5784') is the mountain at the east side of the basin. Cross Commonwealth Creek in the middle of the basin and ascend through trees to the prominent flat area south of the peak. Avoid the large obvious avalanche slopes which extend from valley floor to sum-

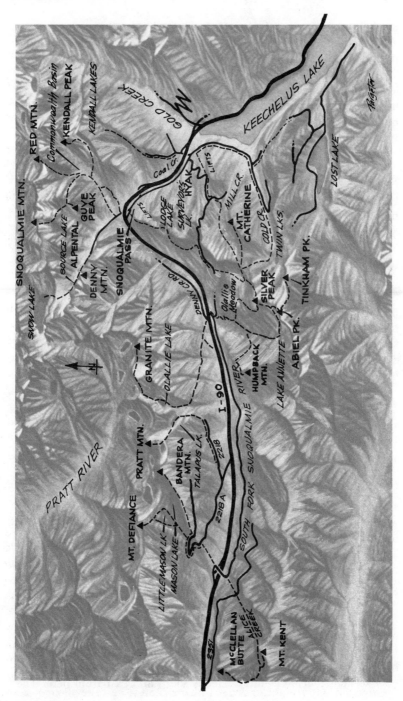

mit left — north — of the heavily forested hillside. If the slopes above are unstable, retreat. The route leads up the slopes to a steep gully to the right — east — of the summit. Leave snowshoes or skis when no longer needed. The last 200 feet or so involves ascending steep slopes left of the gully, which require ice axes and possibly rope. Cornices are usually extensive on the ridge running east from the summit. South of the "flat" and 200 feet lower is the highest of the three **Kendall Lakes.** If the upper slopes of Kendall are unstable, a side trip to these would be a good alternative.

A better approach to these lakes is to park at the plowed area at Hyak exit, or, if that area is full, arrange parking at Hyak Ski Area. Follow logging roads north along Coal Creek as far as possible. Steep, timbered slopes along the creek lead to the first lake at 4400 feet; the highest lake is about 350 feet higher and ¼ mile beyond. The route looks out over Lake Keechelus before entering lovely hemlock and fir forest. The lakes lie beneath the steep peaks of Kendall Ridge.

Several tours are possible from Alpental Ski Area west of Snoqualmie summit. The valley floor is nearly level, climbing gently through heavy timber to tiny **Source Lake** (3760'). Above here, where the timber ends, is an area of very high avalanche hazard. Slides from Chair Peak at the head of the valley, and others, are frequent and deposit in the Source Lake meadows. Camps should be made well back in protective forest.

The steep rise beyond Source Lake leads to a pass (4400'); **Snow Lake** (4016') is just beyond. This slope is avalanche-prone; ascend in timber to the north, and if there is a chance of unstable snow, turn back. The view of snow-covered Snow Lake with Chair Peak above is worth the hike only if conditions are safe.

The area south of Snoqualmie Pass is occupied by the several ski areas, and snowshoers are not particularly welcome. However, by skirting around the congested slopes, one finds a delightful touring and wandering area extending along the Cascade Crest 4-5 miles. The terrain is less rugged than north of Snoqualmie summit, but the views are still excellent.

Park at Snoqualmie summit or Hyak. From the summit, ascend past the Summit Ski Area on either the west or east. Traverse on the west side of the knob which rises about 750 feet above the pass and is the upper terminal for several lifts. This is the slope which avalanches onto the west snowshed, so beware of unstable snow. Beyond Beaver Lake, which is in the ski area, follow the Cascade Crest Trail route into heavy forest and down a steep 500-foot descent to **Lodge Lake** (3750').

Excellent touring country extends south and east from here. The

Crest Trail route continues beyond Lodge Lake on steep slopes looking down on I-90 and west toward Granite Mountain. A steep powerline cut and Rockdale Creek crossing brings one to a logging road which comes from Hyak to the east. Rockdale Lake (3540') is slightly east and **Surveyors Lake** (4000') now north and east and Hyak Lake northeast. If Surveyors Lake is the objective, do not descend to Lodge Lake. **Olallie Meadows** (4000'), with Silver Peak just beyond is to the southwest and by following the logging road and Crest Trail may be reached in about 1 mile from Rockdale Lake. From Lodge Lake or other lakes, or the logging road near Rockdale Lake, you may tour toward Hyak through open forest of hemlock and fir, via powerline slash and logging roads. Silver Peak can be ascended from the Meadows.

Fresh, deep powder snow is as soft as velvet.

Olallie Meadows or **Mt. Catherine** (5052') can also be reached from Hyak. Park and skirt around the ski area on the west side. Descend into valley south of Hyak to a powerline cut, and pick a route up Mill Creek southwest to the pass west of Mt. Catherine. Olallie Meadows are west of the pass. Mt. Catherine can be ascended on its west ridge with a good view from the top of the surrounding Snoqualmie Pass peaks as well as Rainier and the Olympics on a clear day.

A loop trip can be made of Lodge Lake, Surveyors Lake, or Olallie Meadows and other points, starting from either Snoqualmie summit or Hyak. The logging road from Rockdale Lake to Hyak can be followed downhill to Hyak easily. Or from Olallie Meadows or Mt. Catherine, descend past Twin Lakes into Cold Creek to the southeast and follow its logging road back to Hyak. This route is more practical for skiers than snowshoers.

DESTINATION	Elevation: Highest or Starting (+)	Elevation Gain	Miles: Round Trip or One Way (*)	Time	Map on Page
Commonwealth Basin (entrance)	3,500	500	2½	4 hours	53
Guye Peak (beware of avalanche control)	5,168	2,168	4	8 hours	53
Mt. Snoqualmie (beware of avalanche control)	6,278	3,300	6	8-10 hours	53
Red Mtn.	5,890	2,890	5	6-8 hours	53
Kendall Peak	5,784	2,784	5	6-8 hours	53
Kendall Lakes	4,800	2,150	6	6-8 hours	53
Source Lake	3,760	560	3	3-4 hours	53
Snow Lake	4,400	1,200	4	4-5 hours	53
Lodge Lake	3,750	750 to lake 500 return	3	3-4 hours	53
Surveyors Lake Olallie Meadows	4,000	1,000	5	5-6 hours	53
(from Summit)	4,000	1,000	10	8-10 hours	53
(from Hyak)		1,350			
Mt. Catherine	5,052	2,402	7-8	6-8 hours	53
return via Cold Creek			10-12	8-10 hours	53

MAPS

Topographic
Snoqualmie Pass   (30-minute)

U.S. Forest Service
Mt. Baker - Snoqualmie National Forest

Other
The North Central Cascades; pictorial relief map by Richard A. Pargeter

Chapter 6

SNOQUALMIE PASS TO EASTON

Climatic changes become more noticeable the farther east of the Cascade Crest one proceeds; drier, colder conditions prevail and trees are adapted to less moisture. Storm intensity generally decreases: when heavy rain or snow at Snoqualmie summit forces winter recreationists back into their cars and east to Stampede Pass or Easton exits, conditions often are acceptable for an outing there. At other times a storm may be so widespread that not only the Cascade Crest, but the entire area from the Yukon to the Rockies to the Sierras is deluged with snow or rain.

Avalanche activity diminishes with decreasing snow depth. But vigilance must remain as high as at the Crest, because statistics show that the small, unobtrusive slides claim as many victims as the massive ones, simply because they are not so obviously menacing.

Gold Creek canyon, which feeds Lake Keechelus east of Snoqualmie Pass, offers a wide range of snow hikes: a gentle valley floor with logging roads for beginners extending north of I-90 3-4 miles, the lake bed and boat launch access road at the head of the lake south of I-90, and high ridges above for the more experienced. Park at Hyak exit if the plowed parking area is not full, or arrange parking at Hyak Ski Area, and cross under I-90 to reach Gold Creek Road in about ½ mile. Most of the forest on the valley floor has been logged; only a few huge fir and cedars remain. However the views of Chikamin Peak at the valley head, Huckleberry left — west — and the escarpment of Rampart Ridge to the east would not be possible in dense forest. Spur roads climb higher and higher on both sides of the valley, but snow mercifully clothes stumps so winter clearcuts appears as lovely, lumpy meadows.

Beyond 5 miles up Gold Creek the frequency of avalanches which reach the canyon floor increase to the prohibitive level for snow travelers. Only during extended periods of clear weather between storms, with freezing nighttime temperatures and warm days, when the snow pack is stabilized and there is no avalanche hazard should trips into these danger areas be attempted.

Alaska Lake (4200') sits in a deep basin across Gold Creek from Alta Peak, with Alaska Mountain to the north. Follow the prominent tributary stream on the west side of Gold Creek, leaving the trail about 5 miles from I-90. Open slopes which avalanche into Gold Creek must be ascended. Ski tourers prefer a route on the west side of Gold Creek, traversing along the sidehill above the creek to these two lakes.

Joe Lake (4624') is in the next side canyon, between Alaska Mountain and Huckleberry Mountain. Leave the Gold Creek valley about 6 miles from I-90, and pick a route, preferably through a strip of timber on either side of the stream which drains the lake, to the 4624-foot elevation in this basin. The scene is spectacular, with rugged Huckleberry above and Chikamin to the east. Avalanche hazard is great.

About 4 miles up Gold Creek from I-90 a prominent side canyon on the right provides a route of sorts to **Alta Mountain** (6250') on the east rim north of Rampart Ridge. The slopes are steep and the danger of avalanche very high on open or sparsely timbered upper slopes. If there is any threat of unstable snow, just enjoy the view from below. If conditions permit, ascend steep forested slopes east to the 4500-foot ridge and follow north ¾ mile to the summit of Alta.

A less risky route with excellent views leads to the south end of **Rampart Ridge.** Take the first logging spur right off Gold Creek Road, about ½ mile, and from it ascend through clearcut to heavy fir and hemlock above. The slope steepens as elevation is gained, and 1 ½ to 2 miles from the valley floor, due east, the crest of the south ridge of Rampart is reached at 4500-5000 feet. To the east are Rocky Run Creek, Lake Lillian and Mt. Margaret, and from this ridge above 5200 feet Mt. Stuart can be seen to the east. Openings in the trees show Lake Keechelus below and Rainier south, and Snoqualmie Pass to the west. Drifts and cornices increase the difficulty as the ridge narrows, and at 5680 feet a deep airy notch, steep gully and rock gendarme bar progress for most parties.

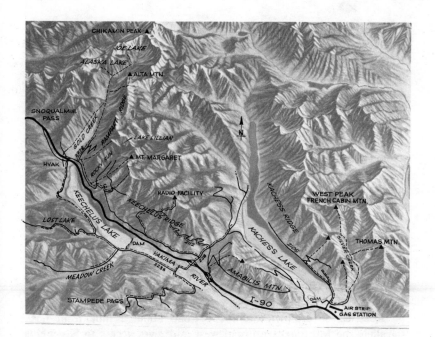

About 2 miles east of Hyak exit via old U. S. 10 is Rocky Run Campground. The gentle slopes and miles of logging roads on **Mt. Margaret** (5520'), the wooded ridge to the north, offer routes for snow travelers of all degrees of experience. The upper slopes and summit have excellent views of Rainier, Stuart, Dutch Miller Gap peaks and the continually increasing clearcuts on neighboring slopes. Most people start on the logging road climbing east from the summer homes east of the campground, picking a way up clearcuts and through the remaining hemlock and fir forest until the ridge east of the false summit is reached. Follow it west — left — and over this 5400-foot point, descending about 100 feet and climbing a final 250 feet over drifts and beside cornices to the summit.

A shorter but more strenuous route starts just north of the summer homes. Follow the ridge on the east side of Rocky Run Creek canyon, then continue up alternately steep and gentle forested slopes, cross a road, more forest, a clearcut, and then continuous forest, partly on a minor ridgetop, to the false summit.

From Hyak a ski tour of approximately 10 miles follows the west shore of Lake Keechelus, then powerline swaths to connect to Road 2238 which is followed to Stampede Pass Road and Overpass on I-90. Keechelus is drawn down during the winter, making possible good touring on the large area of snowcovered lake bottom.

Gentle terrain for beginning snowshoers and ski tourers is readily available both north and south of I-90 at the Stampede Pass-Lake Kachess Overpass, 10 miles east of Snoqualmie summit. Parking is kept plowed for recreationists, both snowmobilers and hikers. At times snow vehicles are a help if they have broken trail where one wants to go. The packed track, however, usually lacks ideal traction for waxes.

Road 228 leads northeast 6 miles to **Lake Kachess.** Spurs on both sides are available for variety and a gentle climb for a better view of the valley and area to the north. Road 2112 forks left in about 1 ½ miles and works its way up **Keechelus Ridge** east of Mt. Margaret. About 8 miles from I-90 is a radio facility. Ability and desire will determine the turnaround spot.

South of the overpass **Stampede Pass** (3700') is reached via the Stampede Pass Road in 5-7 miles, depending on shortcuts under the powerlines; these save considerable mileage but are steeper than the road. Views from Stampede Pass are of the surrounding ridges, valleys and lakes, with Mt. Rainier as a bonus on a clear day. The U. S. Weather Station near the pass is worth a visit.

Road 2238 turns off Stampede Road about 1 mile from I-90, parallels the Milwaukee railroad west and gives access to **Keechelus Dam** in 2 miles, and the west side of the lake for touring. **Lost Lake** (3089'), on Roaring Creek, is about 6 miles from I-90. There is ample gentle terrain south of I-90.

Cabin Creek Overpass, 1 mile east of Stampede Overpass on I-90, opens more roads north and south for touring or beginning snowshoers. Ski racing teams practice here and a ski jumping club has its jumps on the lower slopes of Amabilis Mountain, the wooded ridge east of I-90. Do not carelessly interfere with their activities or destroy their track.

Amabilis Mountain (4554') can be ascended almost anywhere on the side seen from the highway, through moderate to strenuous slopes of hemlock and fir forest, or a new, large clearcut. Clearcuts near the summit, about 2 miles from I-90 provide viewpoints for the distant peaks, and lakes and valleys below. A large radio facility building is on the top, with road access on the northeast side.

The town of Easton is 18 miles east of Snoqualmie Pass. There are several strenuous and some moderate peaks and routes in this area. Silver Creek flows from a very prominent gap in the hills northeast of the town. The peaks or ridgetops which form the drainage basin for the stream are attractive objectives. Arrange parking at the north exit, where there is a service station, or in the town if necessary. The Easton Emergency Airstrip is about ¼ mile off I-90 to the north. It has a plowed lot for snowmobiles. Cross the airstrip and continue toward

Silver Creek canyon, through a powerline cut, avoiding private land at the east end of the airstrip.

A road beyond the airstrip leads to Silver Creek trail about 1 mile from I-90, on the west side of the creek. The trail may be difficult to follow through the narrow gorge when the snow is quite deep; the drop below to the creek is impressive and the steep hillside may avalanche if snow is unstable. The valley opens out in about 1 mile, at 3600 feet. A tributary stream on the east side offers a fairly steep route through fir forest to the 4600-foot ridgetop above. Follow the ridgetop north to the summit of **Thomas Mountain** (5269'), with Lake Cle Elum beyond. Rainier looming in the south, and Mt. Daniels and other Alpine Lakes Area peaks to the north.

The ridge can be followed south about 2 miles, over several minor points to **Mt. Baldy and Domerie Peak** (5107'), named high points on the ridge.

Easton Ridge (4505'), locally called The Old Man's Nose, extends south and east from the entrance to Silver Creek canyon. The powerline north of the airstrip swings under the ridge, providing a roundabout route from beyond the airstrip. A jeep trail follows the abandoned trail for a way at the bottom, circling east, then north behind a knob about

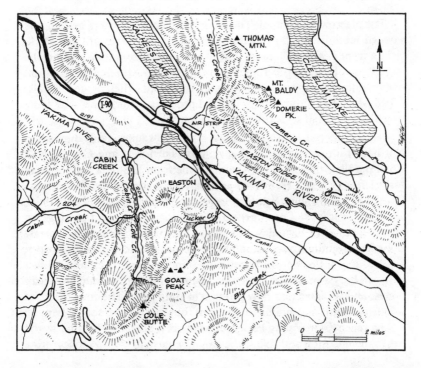

500 feet high. Continue north past the knob on a gently rising bench at 2800 feet and choose a route up the steep, forested hillside above.

By angling up and east from the 2800-foot bench, a flat area, or pass, between Easton Ridge and Mt. Baldy and Domerie Peak can be reached at 3500 feet. This is the head of Domerie Creek, which drains east to the Cle Elum River. The route to The Old Man's Nose follows up the west end of Easton Ridge, reaching the ridgetop at 4291 feet with open areas and views of the lakes and mountains. The 4505-foot "Nose" is about 1 mile southeast along the ridge crest. Several rocky knobs must be climbed over or traversed.

The open fields east of the airstrip are part of a private development. At times it has offered rented snow vehicles for use on this property and the airstrip, which is not plowed in winter. It is an inviting place for beginning ski touring and snowshoeing, but is not ordinarily open to free public use.

South of Easton are several other routes. Parking is usually available in town for these. Local ordinance permits use of snowmobiles on streets, and Cabin Creek Road is heavily used by snow vehicles, as is to lesser extent the canal bank road used for access to Goat Peak. Keep this in mind as you would when walking along any road used by motor vehicles.

The narrow canyon of Tucker Creek makes a deep gap in the wooded foothills south of Easton. The glistening slopes of Goat Peak, visible from I-90 a mile or so east of the town, rise a mile beyond the gap. West of this gap a rounded, wooded peak stands isolated from higher ridges and peaks to the south. Unnamed officially, it is locally called Monahan Mountain (3775') and provides a short hike, with some brush and windfall scrambling to its summit.

Alley Street in Easton crosses both Milwaukee and Burlington Northern railroads; park in this vicinity. Turn west and Cabin Creek Road parallels the railways. About ¼ mile from Easton a logging road forks left off Cabin Creek Road and provides a route through the dense thicket of young conifers. Continue due south across a bench with several powerlines. Continue up steepening slopes to the ridgetop above. The larch, Douglas and grand fir thicket opens into an east slope forest on the strenuous scramble. As always, keep a wary eye open for unstable snow; an avalanche only 6 inches or so deep and 50 feet long can bury a person or slam him against a tree hard enough to break bones, and yet have no really prominent slide path. The view from the wooded summit may not be the greatest, but this is a good short trip.

To reach **Goat Peak** (4981') turn left off Cabin Creek Road at the west side of Easton and follow the canal bank road. At 1 ½ miles, cross the canal on a bridge and continue 1 ½ miles on logging road up Tucker Creek. At about 3100 feet cross the creek to the west and follow a spur ridge that leads to the ridge between the summit rock and several rocky spires on the right, or west. The creek and next 300 feet or so are brushy with dense second growth fir. The remaining 1000 feet are open with a few old burned snags. The view improves with increasing elevation: Lakes Kachess and Cle Elum, with the Dutch Miller Gap peaks beyond Kachess. The Snoqualmie Pass group is west, and Rainier becomes visible as the summit ridge is gained. The rocky summit has a roped pitch near the top and may be climbed most easily via a gully, leading to the base of the rock, which is rather rotten. The former site of a fire lookout is ¼ mile west and is shown as above 5100 feet on U.S.F.S. maps. This is steep country and the slopes avalanche frequently. Recommended time for ascent is early winter, when one can drive up Tucker Creek, or other times when snow conditions are stable.

Other peaks such as **Cole Butte** (5504') may be reached from Cabin Creek valley. The old sawmill community, now summer cabins, is 3 ½ miles by Cabin Creek Road from Easton. Take a left turn and continue up Cabin Creek Road 204 past Boise Cascade re-load 1 ½ miles to Cole Creek Road, which forks left. Continue about 2 miles and again fork left or east on logging road which descends slightly, crosses Cole Creek

Low-country touring.

and angles up through clearcuts in heavy old-growth hemlock, fir, and cedar in creek bottoms, to the 4100-foot pass between Goat Peak and Cole Butte to the south or right. There are many roads — more each year, it seems. From the pass follow the ridge right to the summit.

Cole Butte is a high ridge which forms a 4-mile long "U" around the head of Cole Creek, with several points ranging from 5200 feet to the high point at 5504 feet. The view is much the same as from slightly lower Goat Peak to the northeast. The valleys are deep, slopes steep, and forest on valley floors equal to west slope timber. However, south slopes are more barren and the transition to east slope Cascade pine and sagebrush begins to be evident in this area. Skies are more often blue and temperatures colder.

DESTINATION	Elevation: Highest or Starting (+)	Elevation Gain	Miles: Round Trip or One Way(*)	Time	Map on Page
Gold Creek	3,000+	up to 500	1-8	1-8 hours	53, 59
Alaska Lake	4,200	1,550	12	8-10 hours	59
Joe Lake	4,624	2,000	14	10-12 hours	59
Alta Mtn.	6,250	3,600	12	8-10 hours	59
Rampart Ridge	5,680	3,200	5	4-5 hours	59
Mt. Margaret	5,520	3,000	10	8-10 hours	59
Lake Kachess	2,500	minimal	12	6-8 hours	59
Keechelus Ridge	up to 5,000	up to 2,500	up to 16	optional	59
Stampede Pass (weather station)	3,400	1,000	10-15	6-10 hours	59
Road 2238 and Keechelus Dam	2,521	minimal	6	3-4 hours	59
Lost Lake	3,089	600	12	6-8 hours	59
Amabilis Mtn.	4,554	2,100	4-5	3-4 hours	59
Thomas Mtn.	5,269	3,064	10	6-8 hours	59, 61
Mt. Baldy and Domerie Peak	5,107	2,907	10-12	8-10 hours	61
Easton Ridge (The Old Man's Nose)	4,505	2,305	7-8	6-8 hours	61
Goat Peak	4,981	2,800	5-8	6-10 hours	61
Cole Butte from re-load	5,504	3,305	12-13	8-10 hours	61

MAPS

Topographic

Snoqualmie Pass	(15-minute)
Kachess Lake	(15-minute)
Easton	(15-minute)

U.S. Forest Service
Wenatchee National Forest

Other
The North Central Cascades; pictorial relief map by Richard A. Pargeter

Chapter 7

SALMON LA SAC ROAD
TO FISH LAKE

The terrain in this valley ranges from almost foothill character beside Lake Cle Elum to dense forest, high peaks, and heavy snowfall only 10 to 15 miles north. Salmon la Sac (locally known as "the Sac") seems to be at the line of transition from steep slopes and high avalanche hazard near the Cascade Crest to gentler slopes and less snowfall. There are avalanches off the peaks near the lake, but these do not compare with the major slide paths near Cooper Lake and from Davis Peak and others on the Fish Lake Road.

There are no longer any permanent residents at Salmon la Sac, and the store and cabins have been burned and the site smoothed by bulldozer. During seasons of light snowfall one can often drive to Salmon la Sac all winter, but under normal conditions county snow plows turn around at Driftwood Acres, near the lower end of Lake Cle Elum, adding 11 miles to routes formerly adjacent to a plowed road. Sometimes logging operators keep a portion of the road plowed and will not be hauling on weekends, and roads in this area are used frequently by snowmobiles, so trail breaking on foot is seldom a problem. Touring skis make possible distances unheard of on snowshoes and have an enormous advantage on this type of terrain.

The old-timers frequently snowshoed to Fish Lake, 11 miles beyond Salmon la Sac. There was usually a cabin — and someone living in it all winter — as their destination, so they carried light loads, but most of the old cabins have been destroyed and the present-day traveler must carry shelter and food.

There are many roads and peaks with outstanding viewpoints in this area and the long distance from metropolitan centers precludes the crowds on routes at Snoqualmie Pass.

State 2E begins at Cle Elum and extends through Roslyn and Ronald to "the Sac"; it can also be reached from Bullfrog Interchange west of Cle Elum on State 906. Follow the road to Driftwood Acres or beyond, depending on where snow closes it. There are numerous peaks and ridges on either side of the lake, or miles of touring on roads or lake shore, for objectives. Normally lake level is low in winter, creating a vast expanse of nearly level area for touring and beginning snowshoers.

Hex Mountain (5034'), just east of Lake Cle Elum, has good views of the lake and the peaks across it, as well as the Stuart Range to the east and Mt. Rainier to the south. Follow 2E — Salmon la Sac Road — 2 ½ miles north of Driftwood Acres to Newport Creek. Turn right 0.2 mile beyond and continue up Hex Mountain Road about 1 ½ miles. Leave the road at about 3500 feet and follow the ridge (the summer trail route) to the west "peak" of Hex. The summit is ¼ mile east and slightly higher. The ridges and valleys of the Teanaway extend east, with the escarpment of Table Mountain beyond.

Sasse Mountain (5730') is the next high point north of Hex Mountain. Follow 2E 9 miles from Driftwood Acres to Little Salmon la Sac Creek. The summer trail is on the south side of the creek. Use trail if visible; as elevation is gained the slope beside the creek gradually changes to a ridge shape. Continue on ridgetop, which turns south at about 4200 feet, and in ½ mile turns due east with a 5500-foot point ¼ mile away. The summit is ¼ mile beyond, with a 5300-foot gap separating the two summits. The view is much the same as that from Hex.

Jolly Mountain (6443') is north of Sasse on this divide between the Cle Elum and Teanaway Rivers. The site of a former fire lookout, it has a good view, especially toward Cooper Lake and the peaks of the Alpine Lakes Area to the west. On a clear, bright winter day the sight of the gleaming ridges nearby and peaks beyond on the Cascade Crest is well worth the effort of attaining this point. Follow the summer trail route, which begins at Salmon la Sac Guard Station 11 miles from Driftwood Acres on 2E and stays on the north side of Salmon la Sac Creek. At 4200 feet the route crosses the creek and enters a basin where the canyon widens. Climb to ridgetop up gentlest slopes on the left, north of the summer trail route. Slopes here are steep enough to avalanche if snow is unstable. The ridge above curves south, climbs over several points to the summit 1 to 2 miles away.

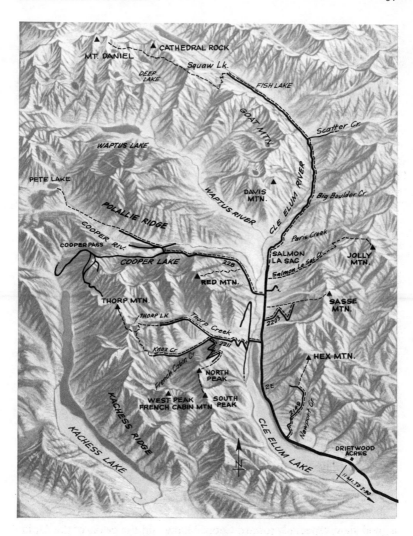

On the west side of Lake Cle Elum are several more good viewpoints. **North and South Peaks of French Cabin Mountain** (5498' and 5569') are accessible from French Cabin Creek Road, which forks left from 2E 7 miles from Driftwood Acres. Follow the road about 3 miles to a left fork at about 3300 feet. Take this spur which descends slightly, crosses the creek, and starts up the ridge leading southeast to the peaks. Continue on road, or shortcut directly to North Peak in about 2 miles.

South Peak is about 1 mile south, with a 5200-foot gap between the two. As on the peaks across Lake Cle Elum, the view is good.

The French Cabin Creek area offers other fine tours. About 1 mile beyond the road fork to North Peak is a tributary from the northwest, Knox Creek. The summer trail follows the north side of the creek to a ridge beyond. **Thorp Mountain Lookout** (5854') is on the far end of this ridge. Check for unstable snow before ascending steep slopes. **Thorp Lake** (4700') is in the basin below and east of the peak. Descend from the 5200-foot saddle in ridge. Lake Kachess is directly below to the west.

A high ridge in the Cle Elum area.

Red Mountain (5722') is a large mass with several summits, west of the Cle Elum River north of Lake Cle Elum. Road 228, 10 miles from Driftwood Acres on 2E, bridges the river and continues west to Cooper Lake. At about 1 ¼ miles, leave Road 228 and ascend timbered slopes to the southeast. At about 4500 feet the aspect changes from broad slopes to ridge, which is followed to the summit. The view is especially noteworthy: Cooper Lake is below to the north with the Lemah-Chimney Rock-Overcoat Peak group beyond, Stuart to the east and Lake Cle Elum and Mt. Rainier south.

Cooper and **Pete Lakes** are two jewels among the scenic treasures of the Salmon la Sac area. Snow-draped Lemah Mountain and Chimney Rock are naturally framed by heavily forested hills as seen from Cooper Lake or the road beyond. There are few lakes or valley bottom settings so perfect for the photographer. The terrain is gentle, with slight elevation gain to these objectives. The greatest hazard is massive avalanches from Polallie Ridge to the north which roar down gullies and pile up on the road beside Cooper, on up to Pete Lake itself. To get to the Pete Lake shelter one must cross a ⅛-mile wide swath which slides so regularly it has no coniferous trees on it and even pushes down trees on the lake's south side.

Road 228 is usually kept packed by snowmobiles. There is a small shelter in the campground at the lower end of Cooper Lake. The long miles and gentle grade suggest skis rather than snowshoes. If time and energy permit, a side trip a mile or so up the road which climbs past the lake on the south to Cooper Pass has excellent views of the lake and the peaks beyond. There is a trail to Cooper Lake, which follows Cooper River from Salmon la Sac, but it is seldom used in winter.

Pete Lake is so hemmed in by heavy timber that the only spot to see Lemah and Chimney is on the lake itself, which is an avalanche deposition area. If there is any slide hazard, this is like looking at Denny Mountain from the top of the snowshed that protects the highway from avalanches west of Snoqualmie Pass on I-90. The trail to Pete begins at the end of Road 228, descends slightly, then wanders among the huge hemlock and fir trees in an almost level grade to the lake. There is touring country here, but the miles of unplowed road which must be travelled create a problem. Early winter, before Road 2E is snowed shut, or a winter with little lowland snowfall are the best times to use these routes.

On rare occasions an early snowfall will cover the very high country with several feet of snow, yet leave access roads clear. **Mt. Daniel** (7960') the highest peak in the Alpine Lakes Area, is a practical objective when one can drive to the trail start at Mosquito Creek, about 3 miles beyond

Fish Lake. The mountain is located on the Cascade Crest behind
Cathedral Rock, as seen from Fish Lake, 11 miles beyond Salmon la
Sac. Many avalanche chutes descend from Cathedral to Deep Lake,
southeast of Daniels. As the route crosses these slopes, it is imperative
that there be no unstable snow above. Every few years in early October
the proper conditions exist for a few days, requiring snowshoes from
Squaw Lake to Daniels. Snowshoes are practical for all but a short
pitch at the top of Daniel's summit, and East Peak. However, the fairly
steep, smooth slopes must be stable and not in danger of avalanching.

Fish Lake valley is an objective for a 3- or 4-day ski tour starting
from Driftwood Acres. It is 22 miles to Fish Lake, but the scenery is
ample reward. Keep in mind the avalanche chutes of Davis Peak and
Goat Mountain on the left beyond Salmon la Sac. These pile up on the
road, especially near Boulder Creek and from Scatter Creek on.

DESTINATION	Elevation: Highest or Starting (+)	Elevation Gain	Miles: Round Trip or One Way (*)	Time	Map on Page
Hex Mtn. (from Road 2E)	5,034	2,640	6-7	6-8 hours	67
Sasse Mtn. (from Road 2E)	5,730	3,385	8	6-8 hours	67
Jolly Mtn. (from Road 2E)	6,443	4,100	10	7-10 hours	67
North Peak French Cabin Mtn. (from 2E)	5,498	3,150	10	6-8 hours	67
South Peak French Cabin Mtn. (from 2E)	5,569	3,250	11	7-9 hours	67
Thorp Mtn. Lookout	5,854	3,500	14	8-10 hours	67
Thorp Lake	5,200	2,855	12	6-8 hours	67
Red Mtn.	5,722	3,377	7	6-8 hours	67
Cooper Lake	2,900	450	10	5-7 hours	67
Pete Lake (from Cooper Lake)	2,980	200	9	4-6 hours	67
Mt. Daniel	7,960	4,610	15	8-12 hours	67

MAPS

Topographic

Kachess Lake	(15-minute)
Mt. Daniel	(7½-minute)
The Cradle	(7½-minute)

U.S. Forest Service
Wenatchee National Forest

Other
The North Central Cascades; pictorial relief map by Richard A. Pargeter

Chapter 8

THE TEANAWAY AND U.S. 97 SOUTH OF INGALLS CREEK

Winter transforms this region of dusty ridges and valleys devoted to commercial logging and road-accessible recreation to first-rate snowshoe hiking and ski touring country. Snowfall is much less than on the Cascade Crest, which also means that frequently a sunny outing can be enjoyed here when the more beautiful trips farther west are stormed in.

Forest cover contrasts sharply with that of the Cascade Crest and its nearby valleys with their huge trees. South slopes have some lovely ponderosa pine, but logged slopes do not reseed well and are generally rather sparse. North slopes and creek bottoms often have thick growths of brush and small trees — mainly Douglas fir, tamarack and grand fir. There are many roads and little need to crawl through these thickets on snowshoes or skis. Snowshoe hare abound in this area, and deer, elk, coyote and bobcat tracks are noted also.

The Teanaway valley offers many gentle miles for ski touring and snowshoe hiking, as well as access to peaks and other points of interest just south of Mt. Stuart. There is real avalanche hazard in the upper Teanaway.

The Teanaway Road forks north of U. S. 97 6 miles east of Cle Elum. The North Fork is generally plowed at least 9 miles to Lick Creek, 6 miles south of Stafford Creek. In winters of light snowfall, plows run another 4 miles to present end of blacktop at Jungle Creek. There are numerous spur roads off the North, Middle and West Forks;

many of these will be packed by snowmobiles. Roadside parking is permitted except when county crews are clearing snow. The best time to attempt the peaks south of Stuart is in early or late winter, when the road is open at least to Stafford Road 2226 (2728').

Navaho Peak (7223'), just west of Three Brothers, is approached from Stafford Road. Note that Stafford Creek forks north off the main canyon about 2 miles from North Fork Teanaway Road. Continue up Stafford Creek 3 ½ miles where the creek forks in the wide upper valley. Pick a route north up the righthand hillside to the ridge above, which is followed east to the summit. If snow on this hillside is unstable, do not continue. (A lower summit about 1 mile southeast is often mistaken for this peak.) The view from the summit includes the Enchantments, which are north across Ingalls Creek, and as far south as Adams when it is clear.

A late winter trip, especially good for skis, is the tour of Stafford Creek, climbing both Navaho and Earle Peaks. Snow must be stable on the east side of Earle; it avalanches very often. However, the ski run off Navaho is good, and the run off Earle's steep and open east side is better. There is a fine route on the south side of Stafford Creek down to 4800 feet.

Miller Peak (6460') is reached by continuing to the end of Stafford Road ¾ mile beyond Stafford Creek canyon. The Miller Peak trail follows Miller Creek about 2 miles, crossing several times, to a basin at 4000 feet where the valley bends with steep slopes beyond. Here the trail climbs southeast through forest to a slight pass or gap in the ridge beyond at 5400 feet. Follow the ridgetop, bypassing a few rocky points on the north, to the summit about a mile northwest.

A possible alternative is to cross Miller Creek and ascend the ridge east of it, over a false peak southwest of the 5400-foot pass. Some rocky outcrops may have to be bypassed. Beware of unstable snow on steep sections of this route. The best view is to the south, across the Teanaway valley to Rainier; only the tops of the Stuart Range peaks show above Navaho and Three Brothers.

Earl Peak (7036') is the high point west of Navaho. Follow North Fork Teanaway Road 2 miles past Stafford Creek, then fork north, or right, on Beverly Creek Road 2110 to its end in 1 ½ miles. Follow Bean Creek east from here, 1 ½ miles with three large avalanche chutes from the north, to where the valley opens out. The gullied west side of Earl Peak rises to the east, with a severe slide hazard. South of the large gully leading to a pass south of the peak is a wooded hillside which provides a safer route to the ridge south of the peak. Two small steep open sections in the forest on this slope give evidence of avalanching.

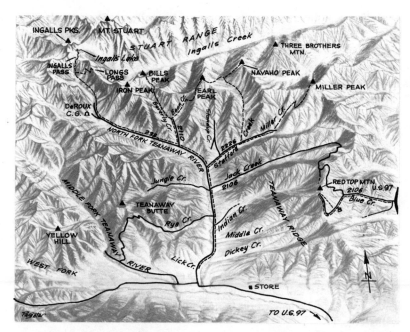

Follow the ridge with large cornices on the east side north to the summit. The view of Stuart is better than from Navaho, and the Enchantments are seen from a slightly different angle.

The valley of Beverly Creek is reached by crossing Bean Creek at road end and following Beverly Creek north. The valley opens out in about a mile with Bills Peak directly ahead. Fourth Creek Pass is to the right, 4 ½ miles, and Turnpike Pass to the left of this peak. The east side of the upper Beverly Creek valley avalanches often. There are pleasant hikes without ascending Bills Peak, which is defended by active avalanche gullies on the east and west and requires very firm snow for a safe ascent.

Ingalls Lake (6463') is a spectacular objective in early winter when North Fork Teanaway Road is free of snow to its end, but often there are 2 or 3 feet of snow at the lake. Follow the trail through **Ingalls Pass** (6480') 2 ½ miles to the lake, with Mt. Stuart and the Ingalls Peaks towering above it. Ingalls Pass and **Longs Pass** (6200') to the east are excellent scenic hikes in themselves; the view is fine to the south to Rainier as well as the peaks near the lake. Ingalls Peak (7664') can be climbed fairly easily when there is just a dusting of snow on it.

If one can arrange snowmobile transportation to road end in midwinter, or take the time to walk the 15-20 miles of snow-covered road, the scenic rewards are exceptional. Avalanche hazard is high, with several slide paths crossing the road near its end, as well as a multitude off the steep slopes near the passes and peaks. Determine that snow conditions are stable before blundering into steep areas.

Blewett Pass summit (4102')is a center for winter recreation. An area is plowed there for parking. **Diamond Head** (5900'), the layered basalt promontory south of the pass, is an excellent viewpoint; it extends south about 5 miles as the high escarpment named Table Mountain.

Follow Swauk Meadows Road 2107 (heavily used by snowmobiles) south from the pass. A 5000-foot bowl, or bench below Diamond Head can be reached by leaving Road 2107 about a mile from U. S. 97. Climb through open forest east or left of the road. The view improves as elevation is gained, and Stuart and Rainier soon appear to the west. The bowl is a good turnaround, although climbers may choose to ascend to the top of Diamond Head above. Steep gullies on the west are the most feasible routes; ice ax and crampons may be necessary. There is rockfall danger in the gullies and on the crumbling cliffs. Another route leads up open slopes on the east side of Diamond Head. High winds often drive clouds of powder snow across the summit. There is avalanche hazard on both east and west sides when the snow is unstable.

A long easy route via Swauk Meadows Road continues south and joins Liberty-Beehive Road 2100, which climbs to the top of Table Mountain, south of Diamond Head. Skiers often prefer a shortcut which leaves Swauk Meadows Road beyond the Meadows, climbs to open slopes and traverses back to Road 2100 as it reaches the top.

Touring and hiking north of Blewett Pass is popular on Scotty Creek Road 223, or on a logging road which forks west off 223, and continues 3 ½ miles. Good views of Stuart. Other roads forking off U. S. 97 south of the Pass can be explored also.

Swauk Campground, 3 ½ miles south of Blewett Pass, is in an ideal area for beginners on snowshoes or skis. There is usually parking at the campground turnoff or ½ mile south at Hurley Creek Road or old U. S. 97 turnoff. The terrain north of the highway is gentle, with roads wandering through the forest and along the streams. Immediately south of the campground is **Sculpture Rock** (3400'), a mere ½ mile and 300-foot climb away. Considering that this point is virtually on the valley floor, the view from this sandstone outcrop is excellent: the ridges rimming the Swauk from Diamond Head to the east, Castle Rock north, and Red Top Lookout in the west. The more energetic may tour or hike beyond to gentle country where other sandstone towers add interest.

Castle Rock (4675') can be approached via the canyon north of Swauk Campground. Follow an old road ¾ mile where the gentle

canyon steepens with an open slope on the right; formerly a small ski area. Ascend to the ridge above and continue to the rock, which has a good view over the entire Swauk with Rainier in the distance. The rock is loose and fractured, and the west "peak" has a route on its north side which is tricky when snow-covered.

By circling past the rock on the north, one can follow the ridge Castle Rock is on, west through some thickets to the original Blewett Pass, and return to the starting point by following old U. S. 97 to its junction with present U. S. 97.

Old Blewett Pass (4064') is a fine objective for beginners on skis or snowshoes. Park as for Castle Rock. The old highway is usually firmly packed by snowmobiles; it reaches the pass in 3 miles. A shorter, steeper and more interesting route is the old pre-highway wagon road. Leave old 97 at Park Creek Campground, ½ mile on the right, and follow the stream on its west side, where several spur roads may lead one away from the stream. In ½ mile these dead end, and only the wagon road continues, more as a trail than a road, to the summit, about 2 miles from U. S. 97.

A loop can be made past Castle Rock in the reverse direction from that previously described. However, even beginning skiers can enjoy returning to their cars via old 97, which is all downhill, gentle and fast, when packed and firm.

Red Top Lookout (5361') is a longer tour to the top of Teanaway Ridge west of Swauk Creek valley and U. S. 97. The summit view includes Rainier, Stuart, and Swauk and Teanaway valleys. Arrange parking at Mineral Springs Resort if there is no space where Blue Creek Road 2106 forks west of U.S. 97 just north of Mineral Springs Campground.

Red Top is another popular snowmobile drive so the trail is usually broken. Follow it toward the Lookout on Road 2106, then left on 2106B toward the summit as far as time and energy permit. A shortcut is possible slightly southeast of the tower. Ascend through a clearcut to the ridge south of the Lookout. The ridgetop road leads north to the tower. The route is ideal for skis as the grade is gentle, yet one can coast a good part of the return.

Other roads which are popular ski touring routes in the Swauk area include Hurley Creek Road 2170 across U. S. 97 from old 97 junction. It runs south, then east, joining Road 2107 in 6 miles, about 4 ½ miles from Blewett Pass. Pipe Creek Road 2129 forks south from U. S. 97 3½ miles west of the pass. Road 2129B forks east beside U.S. 97 and follows the north bank of the creek, 1½ miles to Swauk Meadows, which extend ½ mile or so to Road 2107.

Iron Creek Road 2212 diverges west from U. S. 97 2 ½ miles west of Blewett Pass. Durst Creek Road 2191 forks east off U. S. 97 6 ½ miles from the pass.

Negro Creek, about 2 miles south of Ingalls Creek, has several miles of road touring or hiking, as well as some 7000-foot summits overlooking Ingalls Creek and the south side of the Enchantments. Access to Negro Creek is about 3 miles south of Ingalls Creek. Follow a section of old U. S. 97, now Road 2208, about a mile north to Negro Creek. Shaser Creek, Road 2207, forks west off 2208. Road 2208 continues south to Old Blewett Pass, about 8 miles. Scotty Creek Road 223 forks east off 2208 and continues about 8 miles to "new" Blewett Pass and U. S. 97. Most of these roads are sheltered by timber and ridges above from storm, except at the passes. They are ideal for skis as most slope back to the car, making an easy return. One can make short runs, or overnight excursions, depending on party strength. Several roads fork off U. S. 97 north of Blewett Pass, at Bonanza Campground, Road 2209, and Tronson Meadow on the east, among others.

DESTINATION	Elevation: Highest or Starting (+)	Elevation Gain	Miles: Round Trip or One Way (*)	Time	Map on Page
Navaho Peak (from Stafford Road)	7,223	4,100	9	6-10 hours	73
Miller Peak (from Stafford Road end)	6,460	3,260	6	6-8 hours	73
Earl Peak (from start of Beverly Creek Road)	7,036	3,900	7-8	6-8 hours	73
Ingalls Lake (from end Teanaway Road)	6,463	2,500	6	6-8 hours	73
Ingalls Pass (from end Teanaway Road)	6,480	2,238	3½	3-4 hours	73
Longs Pass	6,200	1,960	3	3-4 hours	73
Diamond Head	5,900	1,800	3-5	4-6 hours	75
Sculpture Rock	3,400	300	2	2-3 hours	75
Castle Rock	4,675	1,625	3	3-5 hours	75
Castle Rock (and Old Blewett Loop)	4,675	1,625	6	4-7 hours	75
Old Blewett Pass (return by old U.S. 97)	4,064	1,000	3 4½	3-5 hours	75
Red Top Lookout	5,361	2,560	16	8-10 hours	73, 75

MAPS

Topographic
Mt. Stuart   (15-minute)
Liberty   (15-minute)

U.S. Forest Service
Wenatchee National Forest

Other
Cross-Country Ski Map of Swauk, by M. Kaatz
The North Central Cascades; pictorial relief map by Richard A. Pargeter

Chapter 9

STEVENS PASS WEST TO INDEX

The Stevens Pass-U.S. 2 area is similar to the Snoqualmie Pass-I-90 region, but Stevens Pass is 1000 feet higher and thus usually has heavier snowfall. This, added to the fact that the ridges and peaks are a little higher, with longer slopes into valleys, results in greater avalanche potential. On the positive side, scenery is often more spectacular at higher elevations, temperatures generally cooler, and snow less sticky. Distances from Puget Sound cities are a little farther than to Snoqualmie, but additional lanes of roadway installed over the summit in recent years facilitate travel.

Low elevation forests are standard for the Cascades — fir and hemlock with some white pine and cedar — changing at higher elevations to the alpine species of the same trees, plus whitebark pine and juniper shrubs.

At Stevens Pass summit hikes to viewpoints are somewhat limited by steep terrain and avalanche hazard. **Skyline Ridge** (5447') just north of Stevens Pass is a short hike up moderate slopes with very good views. Park on north side of U. S. 2 and snowshoe or ski through alpine trees to open slopes above. If snow is stable, continue up past a radio facility at about 4800 feet to Skyline Lake just below the ridge. The energetic may want to scramble ½ mile west to the high point on the ridge. Bypass cliffs on the left and regain ridgetop beyond. Glacier Peak is to the north, the Monte Cristo peaks northwest, Chiwaukums and the Stuart Range are to the southeast.

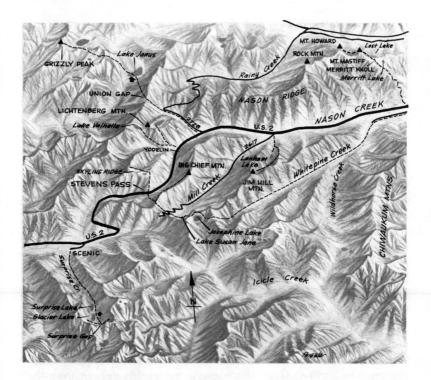

Big Chief Mountain (5858') is due east of the Pass. Park at the summit and skirt ski slopes, climbing southeast to the ridgetop beyond, which is the Cascade Crest. Follow this south until the ridge to Big Chief diverges from the main crest (about 5600'). Continue about ½ mile over a 5675-foot point with a slight descent beyond, to the summit. The view is excellent.

Susan Jane and **Josephine Lakes** (4595' and 4681') lie 4 and 5 miles south of the Pass on the Cascade Crest Trail. There are some avalanche chutes on the trail route, mostly at and near the lakes and under the powerline swath. This is a pretty hike, with two uphill sections going to Josephine. Skirt the ski area and follow the Crest Trail south to a 5100-foot pass through the Crest ridge. Descend on east side to a bench traversing around the head of Mill Creek, which runs east. There are some steep slopes above the route near Lake Susan Jane. An avalanche chute deposits on the lake; do not linger in this, or any other slide path. Climb east to a 5040-foot gap between two high points, which leads to Lake Josephine in a bowl below. Avoid steep slopes and circle left to descend to the flat on the opposite side of the lake. Several short slopes avalanche onto the lake; do not camp in avalanche areas.

Two ski tour loops take off from this route. A powerline road just south of the ridge beyond the summit ski area leads down **Mill Creek,** generally under the electrical lines. The powerline road descends Mill Creek to U. S. 2 about 6 miles east of the pass, where it is designated Road 2617. Experienced and competent skiers can make this route in a day, with the 6-7-mile run down Mill Creek on a road of sorts.

A second route, longer and involving at least one overnight camp, continues east from Lake Josephine, descending **Whitepine Creek,** then Wildhorse Creek Road to Merritt, 16 miles east of Stevens Pass on U. S. 2. Distance from Josephine to Merritt is about 12 miles — 6 miles of trail and 6 miles of road. Skiing down a trail with overnight packs is for experienced skiers. Transportation must be arranged to return to Stevens Pass.

Surprise Creek valley extends south from Scenic, west of Stevens Pass on U. S. 2. Surprise Lake (4500') and Glacier Lake (4800') are reached by trail in 4 and 5 miles from the highway. A shelter at 5000 feet just beyond Glacier Lake makes a good base camp for an overnight trip with objectives near Surprise Gap (5800') 1 mile beyond Glacier Lake. The view south from the Gap is of the Mt. Daniels area. For a better view climb Surprise Mountain (6330'), just west of the gap, or an unnamed 6494-foot point to the east, overlooking the Icicle and Chiwaukum country. There is little slide hazard on the trail until the approach to Surprise Gap, where several avalanches deposit from the peaks on either side of the valley. If there is danger of unstable snow sliding, make the shelter the turnaround, and do not risk the climb beyond Surprise Gap on either peak.

One mile east of Skykomish **Beckler River Road 280** turns off U. S. 2 to the north. Several peaks nearby provide excellent viewpoints, and logging roads extend for miles at gentle grade for touring and hiking. Forest cover is heavy, slopes are moderate, with less obvious avalanche hazard than the long, open mountain slopes a few miles east of Stevens Pass.

Eagle Rock (5612') rises on the west side of the valley about 4 miles from U. S. 2. The approach is via Road 2632 which forks west from Road 280 about 1 mile from U. S. 2. Drive or walk it north of Eagle Creek, about 3 miles. Leave the road and ascend slopes leading northwest to the summit above, about 2-3 miles from Road 2632. The view is excellent: Baring Mountain and Merchant Peak directly west, the Monte Cristo peaks north, and more peaks in every direction.

Beckler Peak (5062') and **Alpine Baldy** (5200') are directly east of Road 280 and north of U. S. 2. Turn north off U. S. 2 onto Road 263 about 4 miles east of Skykomish. Both peaks can be climbed from the

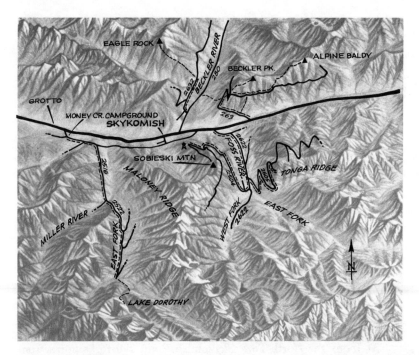

road, which follows a very long, gentle route west, then forks east as Road 2685, climbs up toward Beckler Peak and wanders east across the south side of the peak to its end on the slopes of Alpine Baldy near 4200 feet. Either follow these roads, leaving Road 2685 at 2800 feet and ascending the west ridge to Beckler summit or work out a more direct route from near U. S. 2, by going directly up to Road 2685 near the 2800-foot elevation. It is also possible to leave Road 280 just north of the Beckler River bridge and ascend east directly to Road 2685 and continue to Beckler Peak as described.

A shortcut to Alpine Baldy ascends directly from Road 263 northeast on either side of a knoll near the highway. Cross powerline swath, and continue up forested slopes, regain Road 2685 and follow it to its end (about 4200 feet). Skirt west around an open slope above if snow is unstable, gain the ridge beyond and continue over a 5000-foot point to the summit ½ mile east. The view is excellent.

Barclay Lake (2422') is nestled beneath Mt. Baring's awesome north wall. The trail route is gentle, although logging has disrupted it in places. Views south to Mt. Index are great from the logging clear cuts, and the spires of Merchant Peak are visible to the north farther along the trail. Turn off U.S. 2 at Baring, cross railroad, go through town, under powerlines; follow logging road from Baring, 4½ miles from U.S. 2

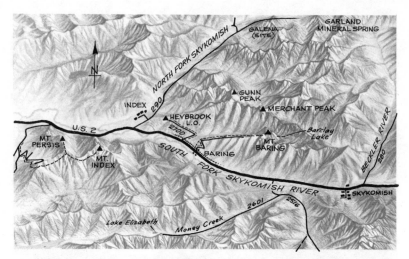

to trail to lake. Road may be closed by snow the entire distance, or just part way. The trail leaves the road on the left, reaches the lake in about 1½ miles. The route follows Barclay Creek the last 3 miles to the lake; there is a shelter at the lower end. Avalanches from Baring's nearly vertical wall above pile up on the lake.

At Index the **North Fork Skykomish Road 290** forks north from U. S. 2. The low elevation of the valley floor often permits driving several miles in winter. The points of interest listed are at valley bottom. The site of Galena, a former mining town, is about 9 miles from U. S. 2 and on the north side of the stream, reached by Road 282.

Garland Mineral Spring, a natural hot spring, is about 5 miles beyond Galena on Road 290. It is delightful to be immersed in hot water with snow on the ground a few feet away. The scenery is beautiful in the valley, and beckoning side roads fork both left and right every few miles.

Holding similar appeal are **Foss River Road 2622** which leaves U. S. 2 south about a mile east of Skykomish, and **Miller River Road 2615,** also south of U. S. 2 just east of Grotto. Both have miles to tour, and when the snow is stable, a strong party can continue on trails beyond. Foss River Road leads to logging roads high on Sobieski Mountain and Tonga Ridge, excellent viewpoints rising west and east of the stream valley. East Fork Miller River trail continues 5 miles or so toward Lake Dorothy in the Alpine Lakes Area before avalanche hazard threatens.

Heybrook Lookout (1701') overlooks the town of Index from a ridge to the east. It is reached in about 2 miles via Road 2700 which forks north off U. S. 2 some 4 miles east of town (the road is gated just off U. S. 2). The view of Mt. Index is most impressive from here.

Mt. Persis (5452') is west of Mt. Index and directly south of U. S. 2. Turn south off U. S. 2 6 miles east of Gold Bar on a logging road just east of No Name Creek. Follow the road, driving when possible as far as 3 miles. Take left forks at intersections as the road heads west along the base of Persis. Ascend the west slopes toward the summit ridge; the short open slopes may avalanche if snow is unstable. The summit is ½ mile south and east of a false summit (4974'). The west side of the peak is large and several approaches are possible; do not go too far east, near a wide expanse of avalanche slopes on the south side of the summit.

Beware of avalanches — even small ones are dangerous.

Experienced mountaineers have traversed the ridge south and east to **Mt. Index** (5979'), over 2 miles away. Several knobs must be traversed around where the ridge crest is at times too narrow to follow. Snow conditions must be firm and crampons and ice ax will likely replace snowshoes. The safest way down from Index summit is to retrace the route over Persis. Descent routes off Index past Lake Serene are steep and hazardous. Allow 3-6 hours round trip from Persis to Index. A camp high on Persis is recommended in preference to making the entire trip from U. S. 2 over Persis to Index and return in one day.

DESTINATION	Elevation: Highest or Starting (+)	Elevation Gain	Miles: Round Trip or One Way (*)	Time	Map on Page
Skyline Ridge	5,447	1,400	2-3	5-7 hours	79
Big Chief Mtn.	5,858	1,800	4	5-6 hours	79
Susan Jane Lake	5,300	1,250 to lake 700 return	9	6-8 hours	79
Lake Josephine	5,300	1,700 to lake 1,200 return	10	1-2 days	79
Mill Creek	5,300	1,250	9*	1-2 days	79
Whitepine Creek	5,300	1,700	18*	2-3 days	79
Surprise Creek Valley (to Surprise Gap)	5,800	3,600	13	2 days	79
Beckler River Road 280	1,200+	optional	optional	optional	81
Eagle Rock	5,612	4,612	11	8-10 hours	81
Beckler Peak	5,062	3,862	6-8	6-10 hours	81
Alpine Baldy	5,200	4,000	8-10	all day	81
Barclay Lake	2,422	1,500	6	8-10 hours	82
North Fork Sky-komish Road 290	800+	optional	optional	optional	82
Foss River Road 2622	1,000+	optional	optional	optional	81
Miller River Road 2615	900+	optional	optional	optional	81
Heybrook Lookout	1,701	900	8	4-5 hours	82
Mt. Persis (from 1,000' elevation)	5,452	4,452	10	8-10 hours	82
Mt. Index	5,979	5,000	15	10-12 hours or 2 days	82

MAPS

Topographic

Index	(15-minute)	Grotto	(7½-minute)
Skykomish	(7½-minute)	Baring	(7½-minute)
Stevens Pass	(7½-minute)	Blanca Lake	(7½-minute)
Scenic	(7½-minute)	Evergreen Mtn.	(7½-minute)
Labyrinth Mtn.	(7½-minute)		

U.S. Forest Service

Mt. Baker - Snoqualmie National Forest
Wenatchee National Forest

Other

The North Central Cascades; pictorial relief map by Richard A. Pargeter

Chapter 10

STEVENS PASS EAST
TO LAKE WENATCHEE

The climatic contrast between the east and west slopes of the Cascades at Stevens Pass is quite similar to that already described at Snoqualmie Pass. Of greater interest to the snow traveler will be the elevation differences between the two areas: in general the ridges and peaks east of Stevens are about 1000 feet higher than those east of Snoqualmie. Cooler temperatures and better snow for traveling can be expected.

The mountain scenery is more varied, with Glacier Peak assuming as prominent a place in the north as Rainier in the south for Snoqualmie, although Rainier is also sometimes in sight. Generally the impression is that there are more mountains visible from the high points above U.S. 2 than are seen from the viewpoints above I-90. Less Puget Sound smog drifts through Stevens than through Snoqualmie Pass and the air here is clearer.

Tree types change as precipitation decreases east of the Crest, ponderosa pine appearing near Lake Wenatchee. However, the mountainous aspect of U.S. 2 continues many miles east of Stevens Pass, through Tumwater Canyon to Leavenworth. The whole area must be given top rating over any other in the State for snow and weather conditions and variety of hikes with excellent scenery.

There is high avalanche hazard on slopes immediately east of the summit, decreasing somewhat farther east. Yodelin development, with cabins concentrated in avalanche deposition areas, was the site of slides in March 1971 which crushed a number of cabins and killed several people. Snowfall is heavy from Stevens Pass to Leavenworth; the danger of sliding snow is general throughout this area.

Stable snow is necessary for a safe ascent of **Lichtenberg Mountain** (5844'). Early winter, before the hazard builds up, late winter, or spells of prolonged clear, cold weather are required. Park near Yodelin and head north toward the peak. The east portal of the first Great Northern railroad tunnel, now abandoned, is in the flats below the development. Cross the flats along Nason Creek and pick a route up the moderate to steep slopes, staying in the forest and avoiding open areas, toward the summit. There are mountains all around but the peaks on the west end of Nason Ridge to the east are most impressive. Continue past a false summit (5732') to the summit ¼ mile beyond.

Lake Valhalla (4830') ½ mile west, can be reached by following Nason Creek valley south of Lichtenberg across from the Yodelin Ski Area. Follow the second tributary stream from the north through the forest (steep in places) to the lake. If there is unstable snow, do not hike in this area as avalanches slide onto the lake, and onto parts of the approach. There is gentle terrain for beginners for touring and hiking along Nason Creek.

Smith Brook Road 2728, about 5 miles east of the summit, gives access to an equally scenic area with much less avalanche hazard, although the first mile has definite slide danger. **Lake Janus** (4146') and **Grizzly Peak** (5593') are just two points of interest 6½ and 11 miles respectively from U.S. 2. A side trip on a logging road climbs northeast out of Smith Brook canyon, through a 4600-foot pass in Nason Ridge, then descends Rainy Creek and the Little Wenatchee River to Lake Wenatchee; a possible ski route. On either side of the pass are peaks rising over 5000 feet — possibly excellent viewpoints.

Union Gap, a pass in the Cascade Crest, is reached 4 miles from U.S. 2. Here the Smith Brook trail joins the Crest Trail; 2½ miles north is Lake Janus. The forest has openings with views from time to time. There is a shelter at Lake Janus which makes a good camp for spending several days in this area.

Beyond Lake Janus 1½ miles the route crosses the Crest with excellent views of Glacier Peak north and the Mt. Daniel area to the south. There are more avalanche chutes crossing the trail beyond this point. Soon Glasses Lake appears below the ridgetop route on the right, with Grizzly Peak beyond 4½ miles from Lake Janus. The Monte Cristo group is also visible from the summit of Grizzly.

Lanham Lake (4143') and **Jim Hill Mountain** (6765') are destina-

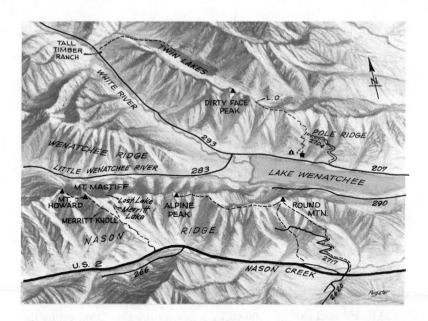

tions up a side canyon on the south side of U.S. 2 a mile east of Smith Brook. The fairly short hike to the lake is a good one for beginners; the climb of Jim Hill involves some real mountaineering technique. Park beside U.S. 2 at Mill Creek Road 2617, 6 miles east of the pass. Cross Lanham Creek on Road 2617 and fork left as trail follows west side of creek. Continue across powerline swath 1½ miles to the lake; take care in a couple of avalanche chutes just before the lake.

To climb Jim Hill, ascend steep timbered hillside east of the lake toward the ridge which leads southeast to the summit ridge. Camp can be made on the hillside. Continue to the summit ridge turn right and follow it southwest to the summit. Bypass a rock outcrop on the right, and scramble over snowy and icy pitches. A 40-foot steep section near the summit probably will necessitate rope protection and a rappel for the descent. The view from the exposed summit is outstanding, from Stuart in the south to Glacier in the north, and beyond.

Across U. S. 2 from Jim Hill and to the northeast are a group of peaks on the west end of Nason Ridge. Merritt Lake, with an unnamed viewpoint above which is called **Merritt Lake Knoll** (6000') for reference here, and **Lost Lake** (4930') are tucked in basins just east of these peaks. **Mt. Mastiff** (6800') and **Mt. Howard** (7063'), the two peaks on the east of the group, have been climbed under winter conditions.

Park beside U. S. 2 about 2 miles west of Merritt and about ¾ mile west of Mahar Creek; the trail starts here and switchbacks from U. S. 2

up steep slopes through open forest of large fir and hemlock, parallel to and west of Mahar Creek to Merritt Lake (in a wooded basin; little view).

To reach the best viewpoint, especially on a one-day trip, stay left of the creek and gain the ridgetop left of the 5000-foot Merritt Lake basin. The ridgetop widens out above 5500 feet, gentling to the "knoll" with groves of trees and the gleaming slopes of Mastiff above. The pointed summit of Howard is left of Mastiff, the Chiwaukums and Stuart Range to the south and Nason Creek valley and high ridges of the Chiwawa and Entiat to the east. Experienced downhill skiers enjoy the steep slopes and widely spaced trees on the return. Climb through a pass 200 feet above and northeast of Merritt Lake and traverse the slopes beyond about a mile to reach Lost Lake; a good camp spot.

There is no avalanche-free route up Mastiff and Howard; ascents of these peaks should not be attempted unless the snow is firm enough for crampons. Ascend north of Lost Lake to the east ridge of Mastiff and follow it west to the summit. There is a steep section from 5800 feet to near the top, where it eases.

Mt. Howard can be climbed by following the ridge connecting the two peaks, descending to a 6300-foot gap between. Stay left of cliffs near the top of Howard when ascending from the gap. Carry ice ax, crampons and rope; these high, wind-blasted ridges are often icy in winter. The views from these airy summits are exceptional, with Rainier in the south and many peaks beyond Glacier to the north.

The Chiwaukum Mountains to the south are high, with several broad, open ridgetops which are attractive to skiers as well as snowshoers. Access is long, but once out of the valleys there is fairly gentle terrain with open forest and exceptional views.

One approach is past **Lake Ethel** (5500') reached by trail along Gill Creek. Park in Merritt, about 16 miles east of Stevens Pass. There is gentle terrain on snow-covered roads nearby for touring or hiking. Lake Ethel trail starts ¾ mile south of Merritt on Road 2734. The first 1500 feet elevation is up a steep slope where the trail may be hard to find. Unstable slopes may slide here. Stay between Gill Creek on the left and another stream on the right, and regain the trail above 3600 feet where it is more easily identified by the typical "lane" through the forest. The slope gentles and the lake is reached in 4 miles more. There are good campsites here. South of the lake the slope rises steeply 1000 feet to a pass. Do not proceed beyond Lake Ethel if snow is unstable. From the pass traverse west, if conditions permit, descending slightly to bypass cliffs, to the broad ridgetop beyond. Loch Eileen is in the next canyon south. There is good touring some distance south toward the 8000-foot peaks of the Chiwaukums, with views in all directions. Cold winds are to be expected here.

Another high ridgetop with excellent views lies southeast a few miles. **McCue Ridge** (to 6288') rises high above Chiwaukum Lake to the south, with Big Jim Mountain southeast and Glacier Peak to the north. The approach via Coulter Creek Road and trail is just about avalanche-free, and only the last hour or so of travel to the top of McCue Ridge is steep and not sheltered by forest. Park beside U. S. 2 at Coulter Creek Road 2629, about 3 miles west of Lake Wenatchee Road. Road 2629 may have been extended, but trail signed Lake Julius formerly began at road end. The trail goes through dense forest, following a broad ridgetop southwest to a junction 5 ½ miles from U. S. 2. McCue Ridge trail forks left; Lake Julius is an interesting side trip 1 mile west through more timber. Head southwest and climb the last steep slope ½ mile to the crest of McCue Ridge, or follow longer and gentler trail route to the west if snow is unstable. The ridge continues west several miles, with groves of whitebark pine providing sheltered campsites. Touring a high, gentle ridge such as this, with its exceptional view, is a rewarding experience.

Nason Ridge, with **Alpine Peak** (6237') and **Round Mountain** (5700') parallels U. S. 2 on the north. The ridgetop view is outstanding: Lake Wenatchee below, the near peaks of Glacier Peak Wilderness beyond, and the cone of Glacier itself, and the Stuart and Chiwaukum ranges to the south. Turn off U. S. 2 about 3 miles east of Merritt at Butcher Creek Road 2717. Follow to road end in 3.7 miles, taking the right fork at 1½ miles and the left at 2½ miles. The trail through open forest reaches the crest of Nason Ridge in 1½ miles, near Round Mountain. Alpine Lookout is 2½ miles west. The highlight of the trip is the scenery in all directions from the ridge. Skis are good on this route as the descent by Butcher Creek Road can be done by less experienced skiers.

There is a shortcut to Round Mountain. Turn off U. S. 2 about 1 mile east of Merritt on a secondary road. Locate parking, pick a route on the west of Road 2717 and ascend directly to the ridgetop above. Beware of unstable snow on the steep, open slopes.

Southeast of the junction of U.S. 2 and the Lake Wenatchee Road rises **Natapoc Mountain** (4204'). Its summit is wooded, but there are open areas from which to enjoy the view of the Stuart range to the south. Arrange parking at the gas station or cafe, or on a shoulder of the Lake Wenatchee Road. Head southeast toward the base of the west ridge of Natapoc. Climb the steep slope at the bottom and follow the ridgetop about 1 mile to the summit. The ridge has steep and gentle

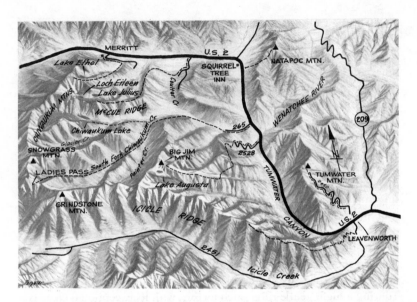

sections and the trees are rather close for ski descents; it is easy on snowshoes.

Chiwaukum Creek provides access to the heart of this range. **Ladies Pass** (6800') is higher than many summits described in this guide; the highest peaks in the Chiwaukums are only about 1000 feet higher. The forest changes from ponderosa pine at the 1800-foot level to fir and hemlock, and as elevation increases, to alpine species at Ladies Pass. For a real backcountry tour, a long hike into the isolation of the Chiwaukums would be ideal.

The route through the valley is protected by high ridges from storms. There are areas of high avalanche hazard where the route lies below high, steep slopes. Early or late winter, or prolonged spells of good weather are essential for safety on this trip. Park where Chiwaukum Creek Road 265 turns south off U.S. 2 just west of Tumwater Canyon. Follow the road to trail start and continue 7 miles from U.S. 2 where the stream forks. (This section of road would be excellent for day trips for beginners on snowshoes or skis.) Take the south fork to the left. The right fork, Glacier Creek, continues to Chiwaukum Lake and beyond, but there is no winter information available at present for this area.

Beware, on the first 1½ miles on South Fork Chiwaukum, of avalanche danger; the trail crosses numerous gullies which carry sliding snow from the ridge above. There are good campsites opposite Painter Creek, 8½ miles from U.S. 2. It is 5 miles from here to near Snowgrass

Mountain on the right, where the forest opens out and one enters the avalanche area which extends to Ladies Pass. It is 2 miles to the pass, and the scattered alpine trees afford little actual protection from sliding snow; retreat if snow is unstable. Snowgrass Mountain is just north of the pass, beyond Lakes Flora and Brigham. To the southwest are the ridges and valleys of the upper Icicle, with Mt. Daniel area beyond. Nearby peaks, Cape Horn and Grindstone Mountain, block the view toward Mt. Stuart.

Big Jim Mountain (7763') is a high point on the east edge of the Chiwaukums and west of Icicle Ridge, which separates Tumwater Canyon from Icicle River. The view is of the Stuart range, as well as north to Glacier Peak. There is avalanche hazard where the trail traverses steep forested slopes around the head of Hatchery Creek. Park where Hatchery Creek Road 2528 forks south from U.S. 2 at the west end of Tumwater Canyon. Follow this road, which is on the west side of the Wenatchee River, to where the trail to Icicle Ridge begins, about 2½ miles. Continue on the trail as it makes the long climb out of Hatchery Creek and traverses east. Beware of unstable snow in this area. The forest changes from deciduous trees in Hatchery Creek to fir and other conifers as elevation is gained. The trail crosses a slight divide into Falls Creek Canyon and the slope gentles. Aspen groves appear about 5500 feet. The trail traverses the head of Falls Creek, crosses the ridge beyond and descends slightly into Cabin Creek. Good campspots here. The trail forks near here, 3½ miles from Hatchery Creek Road, the right fork going to Lake Augusta at the head of this valley. The right hand ridge runs west and is the route to Big Jim, about 1½ miles, the high point above Lake Augusta. Traverse rock outcrops on south side. Hard steep snow may call for ice ax, rope, and crampons. The ridge merges with the upper slopes of Big Jim north of Lake Augusta, then swings south to the summit. The views of Glacier Peak and others to the north, Chiwaukums west, and Rainier southwest are outstanding, but Stuart and the Enchantments across the Icicle are beyond description.

Lake Wenatchee, reached from U.S. 2 via State 207, has been promoted as great snowmobile country. It has lovely scenery and is equally good for foot travel, and there is seldom much trail breaking to do on lowland routes. For those who cannot bear to coexist with motorized traffic, there are many logging roads, as well as gentle terrain near Lake Wenatchee State Park, toward Nason Ridge, which are seldom walked or traveled by machine in winter.

Dirty Face Peak (5989') dominates the north ridge at the head of the lake, with excellent views from the upper ridge and summit. Park at Lake Wenatchee Forest Service Campground on Road 207 and follow the trail 4½ miles to the summit. There are many switchbacks as the trail climbs from heavy fir and hemlock forest to ridgetop just east of the summit. The last ¼ mile is open and steep and may avalanche if the snow is unstable.

An alternative with a gentler grade follows Pole Ridge Road 2704 which joins the trail from about 3350 to 3700 feet. Road 2704 is unmarked at times but forks off Road 207 about a mile east of Lake Wenatchee Ranger Station. The road is a good hike for beginning snowshoers and skiers who do not have the strength or skill to handle the steep upper slopes of Dirty Face. The view of Lake Wenatchee below and Nason Ridge beyond is reward for those who do not make the summit.

At the head of the lake Road 207 forks and continues many miles farther up the Little Wenatchee on the left and White River to the right. Each has a number of side roads to explore. The miles are long but the terrain is ideal for ski touring.

An interesting trip off White River goes to **Twin Lakes** (2825') through the 3000-foot deep gorge Napeequa River has cut through the White Mountains north of Dirty Face. Park at end of Road 207, or if plowed, at Tall Timber Ranch 6 miles from 207 on White River Road 293. The trail follows the south side of Napeequa River. There is avalanche hazard where the trail leads below steep cliffs. The forest is heavy to the gorge, but once beyond and into Napeequa valley the forest thins and one can see out. The first lake is about a mile from the gorge and the second is ¼ mile beyond. The view across the lakes and up the deep, U-shaped valley is most impressive.

Snowplastered trees — a lovely winter sight.

DESTINATION	Elevation: Highest or Starting (+)	Elevation Gain	Miles: Round Trip or One Way (*)	Time	Map on Page
Lichtenberg Mtn.	5,844	2,500	7-8	6-8 hours	79
Lake Valhalla	4,830	1,500	7-8	6-8 hours	79
Lake Janus	4,800	1,500	13	8-10 hours	79
Grizzly Peak	5,593	2,500	22	3 days	79
Lanham Lake	4,143	1,300	3-4	5-6 hours	79
Jim Hill Mtn.	6,765	3,800	8	10-12 hours or 2 days	79
Merritt Lake Knoll	6,000	3,300	7	6-8 hours	79, 87
Lost Lake	6,000	3,300	9	8-10 hours	79, 87
Mt. Mastiff (from Lost Lake)	6,800	1,870	2	4-5 hours	79, 87
Mt. Howard (via Mt. Mastiff from Lost Lake)	7,063	2,800	4	6-8 hours	79, 87
Lake Ethel	5,500	3,300	14	8-10 hours or 2 days	90
McCue Ridge	6,288	4,100	12	10-12 hours or 2 days	90
Alpine Peak (via Butcher Creek Road)	6,237	4,037	16	2 days	87
Round Mtn.	5,700	3,986	11	6-8 hours	87
Natapoc Mtn.	4,204	2,185	5	6-8 hours	90
Ladies Pass	6,800	4,600	28	4 days	90
Big Jim Mtn.	7,763	6,000	18	2-3 days	90
Dirty Face Peak (by trail)	5,989	4,000	9	8-10 hours	87
Twin Lakes (from Road 293)	2,825	800	6.4	6-8 hours	87

MAPS

Topographic

Chiwaukum	(15-minute)
Wenatchee Lake	(15-minute)
Index	(15-minute)
Leavenworth	(15-minute)
Stevens Pass	(7½-minute)
Labyrinth Mtn.	(7½-minute)
Captain Point	(7½-minute)

U.S. Forest Service
Mt. Baker - Snoqualmie National Forest
Wenatchee National Forest

Other
The North Central Cascades; pictorial relief map by Richard A. Pargeter

Chapter 11

CASCADES—WEST SIDE— STEVENS PASS NORTH

The rugged west slope of the Cascades north of Stevens Pass to the Canadian border has probably the most spectacular winter scenery of any area described in this book. Deep, heavily forested valleys with jagged, snowy peaks rising above the foothills are typical. Snow depths increase perceptibly the farther one goes north.

Slopes are consistently steep as one climbs from sheltered valley floor to scenic ridgetop 4000 feet or so above. Heavy snowfall on such terrain creates extreme avalanche hazard on many routes until sun, warm temperatures and several days' time have stabilized it. Storms sufficient to cause so much snowfall precludes more than a few erratically spaced bright sunny days. Snowfall which does not melt in summer in sheltered areas has created an extensive glacier system on the peaks in this area.

Valley bottoms are shaded not only by the high ridges, but by magnificent forests of fir, hemlock, spruce and cedar, changing as elevation is gained to mountain hemlock, Alaska cedar, alpine fir and juniper. Wind, snow and storm keep ridgetop species from growing more than a few feet high.

Access is by roads in the four great river valleys of this section: starting from the south, the South and North Forks of the Stillaguamish, the Skagit and its tributary Baker River, and the Nooksack just south of the Canadian border.

Stillaguamish

The Mountain Loop Highway along the South Fork Stillaguamish River (often called Silverton Road) leads from Granite Falls, which is reached via State 92 from Marysville, north of Everett.

Mt. Pilchuck (5324') just east of Granite Falls, stands abruptly above the rolling Puget Sound country. The view beyond the nearby farms includes Rainier, Glacier, Baker, Vancouver Island, the San Juan Islands, Olympics, Three Fingers and Whitehorse just north. It is a fairly short trip with some moderate slopes.

Drive Mountain Loop Highway 1 ½ miles east of Verlot, turn south on road to Mt. Pilchuck State Park and Ski Area (2800'); parking is normally adequate. From the parking area ascend along the south side of the chairlift — stay off the ski slopes — to the top terminal of the upper chair. Continue to the ridge above, either over or just under, depending on snow conditions, the 4600-foot knoll called "Little Pilchuck." The ridge beyond leads to the summit and even better views. Avalanche hazard is negligible but if snow is hard, rope, ice ax and crampons may be needed for safe travel.

Mountain Loop Highway is plowed to the junction with Deer Creek Road 3016 about 15 miles east of Verlot. The many side roads are especially popular with ski tourers, and several points beyond road ends are favorites of snowshoers and expert skiers. **Schweitzer Road 3015** forks south about 5 miles east of Verlot, swings past Lake Evan, about 3½ miles from the highway, and continues on west. Several spurs leave 3015 in either direction.

About 7 miles east of Verlot **Mallardy Ridge Road 3034** forks south, climbing in about 4 miles to the broad, gentle ridgetop at 3500 feet. Turn right on 3005 at about 2 miles from the highway, and continue as time and strength permit; the view improves.

At the end of plowed Mountain Loop Highway, Deer Creek Road 3016 forks north and extends about 4 ½ miles almost to **Kelcema Lake** (3182'). At road end, cross the creek north and follow trail ½ mile to the lake, in a deep basin below Bald Mountain. Deer Creek Road is closed to snowmobiles and other motorized vehicles in winter.

A more rugged objective is **Helena Peak** (5401'), northeast of Kelcema Lake. The route climbs from the lake to Deer Creek Pass (3700'), through the ridge north, then angles up on the north side of the ridge to the east, provided snow is stable, to a 4400-foot saddle south of the summit. The last steep slopes must be stable for safe ascent and may require ice ax, crampons and rope. Devils Peak is to the south, with Big Four and Monte Cristo Peaks beyond, Three Fingers and Whitehorse northwest, as well as more distant peaks.

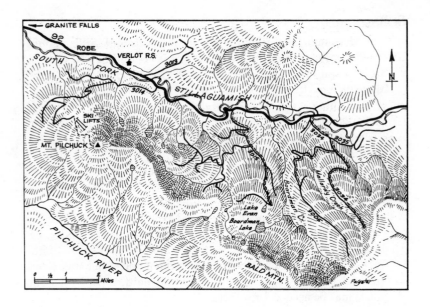

Devils Peak (5453') is approached via the right fork of Deer Creek Road about ½ mile from the highway. The road follows above Deer Creek in heavy timber. About 1 ½ miles from Road 3016 are several switchbacks beside a tributary stream of Coal Creek which descends from a basin east of Devils Peak. Follow this stream to the basin through thinning timber and, if slopes above are stable, ascend to the ridge south of the rocky summit, climbing north to the top. The final slopes are steep and prone to avalanche. Late winter or early spring is best for the ascent. From the summit one sees peaks extending to the horizon in all directions, with Rainier to the south and Baker to the north.

Mountain Loop Highway beyond Deer Creek is quite popular for touring and snowshoeing. Continue toward Barlow Pass as far as time and energy permit. Hall Peak and Big Four Mountain rise spectacularly above the road to the southwest.

Three side roads offer excellent scenery as they climb out of the deep South Stillaguamish canyon. **Coal Creek Road 3006** forks east about 2 miles beyond Coal Creek, just past Big Four Campground. As the road gains elevation there are views of Hall, Big Four and other peaks beyond.

Perry Creek Road 3010 forks east about ½ mile beyond Coal Creek Road, climbs into the Perry Creek canyon above and continues 2-3 miles, with the steep slopes of Mt. Dickerman to the south.

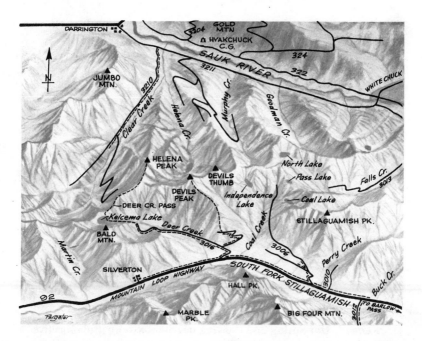

Sunrise Road 3012 forks west off the highway about 1 ½ miles beyond Perry Creek Road and extends south 2-3 miles up a side canyon west of Barlow Pass.

Several very rewarding tours and hikes begin in the deep river valleys east of Darrington, which is reached by State Route 530 east from Arlington. Winter travel to distant backcountry areas is hindered as few roads are plowed. However, there are many, many miles of snowcovered roads for ski touring and snowshoe hiking. Early or late winter dates are best for the more remote of these areas, before heavy snowfall has closed roads in low-elevation valleys, or after it has melted off. Route 530 and the Darrington-Rockport roads are plowed. At present this section of the Cascades is not heavily used for winter recreation.

The county road south of Darrington on the west side of Sauk River is plowed about 2 miles to **Clear Creek Road 3210.** This road, with several spurs, extends about 10 miles and is excellent for ski touring and snowshoeing. There is avalanche hazard beyond Jumbo Mountain from several chutes which funnel down onto the road. There are good views of Big Bear, Liberty, and Helena Peaks and in the upper portion of the drainage are the steep cliffs locally known as Witchdoctor Wall. This road is closed to snowmobiles and other motorized vehicles in winter.

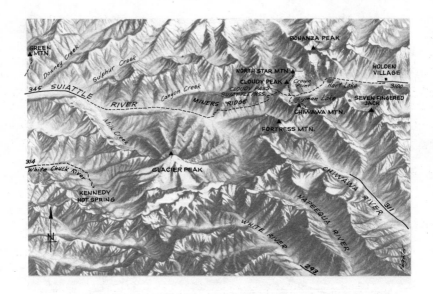

Kennedy Hot Spring and the area nearby is a delightful objective in winter, preferably in early or late winter when one can drive to the end of Whitechuck River Road 314. Follow the Mountain Loop Highway 322 east of Darrington on the east side of the Sauk River about 10 miles and turn east up Whitechuck Road 314.

From road end at 2300 feet a trail with good bridges and footlogs continues through deep forest 6 miles to the hot spring on the west side of the river. As this is a Wilderness Area, the three-sided shelters and guard station are not maintained, and may not exist in the future. The 4 x 6-foot spring is boxed in and the 98°F water is wonderfully relaxing for tired muscles. Odorless gases bubbling through the water give a gentle whirlpool effect. For excellent views of Glacier Peak to the east, continue on Lake Byrne trail ½ mile as it quickly climbs the slope above the spring.

Early winter trips on Suiattle River trail provide spectacular views of Glacier Peak to the south. Drive 10 miles north of Darrington toward Rockport, turn east on **Suiattle Road 345** and continue to road end (1651'). There are several three-sided shelters on the trail, which can be followed 10 miles or more in winter. There is about 1200 feet elevation gain to the junction with Miners Ridge trail to Image Lake. An occasional party goes into the Image Lake area and continues on through to Lake Chelan. However, the avalanche hazard from Image Lake on east is extremely high. See Chapter 13 for more details of this route.

Green Mountain (6500') is approached via Green Mountain Road 3227 which forks north off Suiattle Road 345 about 3 miles east of Buck Creek. Drive this road as far as possible and continue on trail 782. Several humps are crossed before the final summit, with its lookout tower, is reached. There are dramatic views of Glacier, Dome Peak area and Buckindy, as well as many others. This is a strenuous trip, and the entire route above timberline is prone to avalanche.

Many other roads are excellent for ski touring and showshoeing in this area. A quick glance at a Forest Service map will suggest almost unlimited possibilities. Three roads near Darrington are worthy of mention, all of which are closed to snowmobiles and other motorized vehicles in winter.

Round Mountain Road 337 climbs the mountainside north of North Fork Stillaguamish River. Turn north off Route 530 about 5 miles west of Darrington on a county road which crosses the river and swings west. 337 forks north about 1 ½ miles from Route 530. There are excellent views south of Whitehorse Mountain.

Gold Mountain Road 3204 forks east off Mountain Loop Highway east of Darrington at Hyakchuck Campground and switchbacks up the steep mountainside to the east, with views of Whitehorse and Jumbo to the west.

Prairie Mountain Road 3214 is reached via the county road on the east side of the Sauk River about 4 miles northeast of Darrington. The road switchbacks high on the side of Prairie Mountain (5586'). The view is excellent.

Skagit

Access to the area south of Skagit River and northwest of Darrington is somewhat complicated. At Concrete turn south, cross the Skagit on Dalles Bridge and drive east on the county road on the south side of the river. Turn south on Finney Road 353 west of where Sauk River flows into Skagit. The road extends for many miles with spurs on both sides, and eventually connects with Road 337 mentioned in the Darrington section. However, this is a route more suited to motor-driven vehicles than foot travel due to its length. **Finney Creek Shelter,** about 5 miles up Road 353, is a good turnaround, or campsite for an overnight stay. Sauk Mountain Road 3602 forks north at Rockport Park; good for touring and hiking.

Drive east on Highway 20 to Marblemount and continue east on Cascade River Road 3528 which leads along the Cascade River and eventually to the trail to Cascade Pass, a famous scenic area in summer. The avalanche hazard the last miles to the pass in midwinter is too

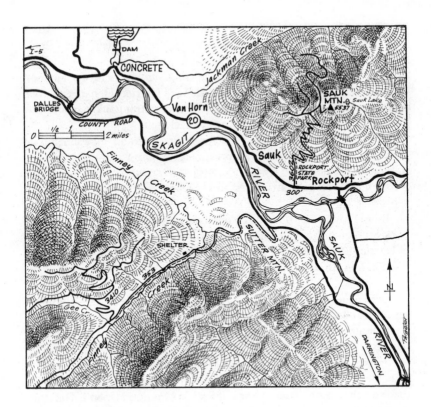

severe to suggest a trip there at that time, although it has been visited in early or late winter when snow conditions were stable. There are miles of road for touring before one arrives beneath the awesome avalanche slopes inside North Cascades National Park a mile or so beyond Mineral Park Campground. Check at Park headquarters at Marblemount before entering this area.

Drive east from Marblemount to Bacon Creek just outside Ross Lake National Recreation Area and turn north on **Bacon Creek Road 3717.** This road and its spurs offer many miles of touring and snowshoeing. Bacon Peak is west of valley floor Road 3717 and Damnation is to the east. Road 3708 forks east and climbs high on the hillside above Bacon Creek, with good views out to the west and south.

A rugged hike to a superb viewpoint on **Sourdough Mountain** north of Diablo Lake begins at the base of Diablo Dam just off Highway 20 about 7 miles east of Newhalem. Park at designated area near powerhouse; trail starts in rockslide 3 blocks past the powerhouse and swimming pool. Often the lower trail is free of snow and snowshoes and

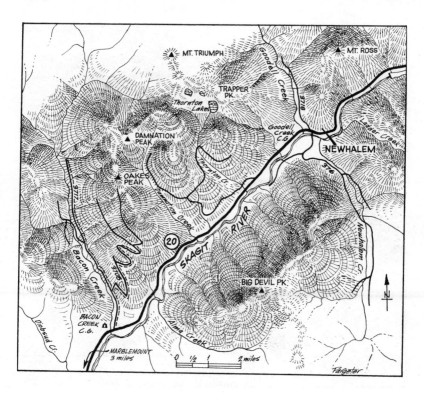

skis may be carried partway. Elevation gain in the first 3 miles is 3500 feet, a steep, tough climb through heavy forest. At this point a ¾-mile spur trail forks west to a TV facility. Good campsites in this area. Continue on up the minor ridge the TV station is located on rather than following the trail route, which crosses slopes which frequently avalanche, to where it joins the main ridge above and northwest of the lookout tower. One may continue to the top of the obvious high point. Across Diablo Lake are Pyramid, Colonial and Snowfield Peaks; up Thunder Creek are Logan, Buckner and Boston, and north are the Southern Pickets. West and far below is Skagit Gorge and east near Ross Lake are Jack and Ruby Mountains.

South of Mt. Baker, the large area near Baker Lake is laced with logging roads and is used extensively for winter recreation by snowshoers, skiers, and snowmobilers. Views of the southeast side of Mt. Baker are exceptionally fine.

Drive east from Sedro Woolley on Highway 20, the North Cascades route. Turn north on Baker Lake Road 6 miles west of Concrete. As the road nears the north end of Lake Shannon, fork left on road 372 and

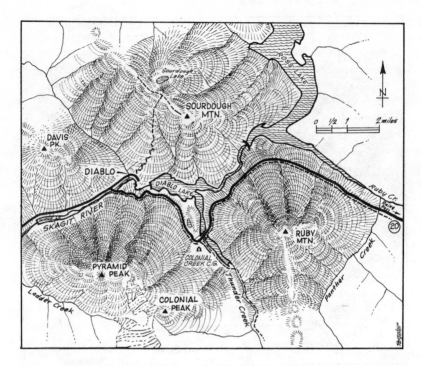

drive to where it is closed by snow. About 6 miles from Baker Lake Road **Dillard Point Lookout Road** turns left to the lookout (2400'), about ½ mile farther. The lookout has a sweeping view over the lakes below, and of Baker, Shuksan, and the peaks south of Shuksan.

Continue to the end of Road 372 where a trail leads in 2 miles to **Schrieber's Meadows** and shelter. This is an especially lovely place with Baker rising high above to the north, and the shelter makes it a wonderful camp spot. The area beyond Road 372 is closed to motorized vehicles year round.

Drive farther north on Baker Lake Road to **Koma Kulshan Guard Station** near Road 3720, which forks right to upper Baker Dam. The gentle flat is an ideal place for beginners to put on skis or snowshoes for the first time and get the feel of the devices on level snow. Shadow of the Sentinels Nature Trail is ½ mile north of Koma Kulshan on Baker Lake Highway. This is a short, rather easy trail through huge old-growth trees.

Cross the river at Upper Baker Dam, drive to end of **Anderson Creek Road 3721,** and follow the trail on the east side of Baker Lake. Tour the road if it is closed by snow.

Drive 3 miles north of Koma Kulshan Guard Station on Baker Lake

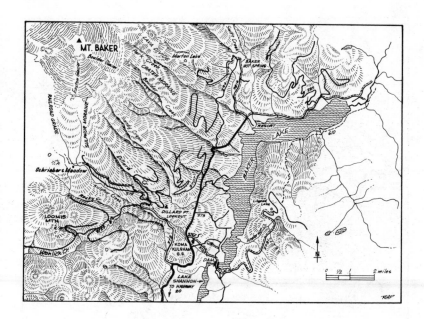

Road and turn left on **Sandy Creek Road 3707.** This road and its spurs extend several miles; good views and good grade for skis.

Baker Hot Spring is at summer road end, but in winter Road 3816 from Baker Lake to the hot spring is normally closed by snow. A 4-6 mile walk and overnight camp may be necessary to enjoy and explore the area. **Marten Lake Road** climbs west from the hot spring toward Marten Lake below Lava Divide above. For a longer trip, or when one can drive to the hot spring, this is a good route for a better view over the area. There are other roads which lead to very scenic areas and enjoyable outings. From road end, trail 610 along the east shore of Baker Lake is an excellent hike.

Highway 20 winter road end is near Diablo. A few parties ski or snowshoe the highway each winter over Rainy Pass and Washington Pass to Mazama in Methow valley. As described in more detail in Chapter 13, there are numerous avalanche chutes which slide onto the roadway. Early in winter, before the section east of Washington Pass avalanches shut to motorized vehicles, many people snowmobile the route, round trip, in a short day. In winters of exceptionally heavy snowfall, even the community of Diablo is cut off by avalanches on Highway 20 in Skagit Gorge. One must never assume that the snow has firmed up so that there is no danger from avalanches in this area of steep mountains and heavy snowfall.

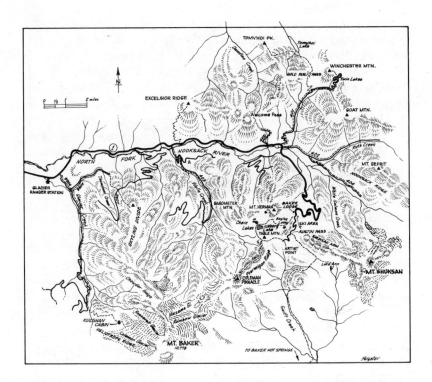

Nooksack

The scenic highlight of winter touring and snowshoeing in the North Cascades is the Mt. Baker area, with its two splendid mountains — Baker and Shuksan — as well as smaller but equally rugged peaks to the east, south and north. Mt. Baker Ski Area at winter road end (4300') has had snow depths close to the records established on Mt. Rainier at Paradise (5400').

Avalanche danger is extremely high and clear days rather few and far between. At times snow is quite stable and peaks such as Tomyhoi, north of Baker, have been climbed during these periods. Anyone unfamiliar with the area must exercise great caution and check with the U. S. Forest Service snow ranger at the ski area, or other rangers at Glacier Ranger Station for advice on avalanche hazards.

Mt. Baker Highway 542 from Bellingham provides access along Nooksack River to this area, about 35 miles to the community of Glacier. Roads fork off both north and south and many are excellent for touring and snowshoeing. Of particular interest is Glacier Creek Road 3904, which turns south off the highway just beyond Glacier, and has miles of excellent snowcovered road with good views south of Mt. Baker. A steep rock face 2 miles from the highway periodically drops rocks and debris onto the road, closing it to vehicle traffic. Park on the north side of the road at a safe distance from the rockfall.

Kulshan Cabin (4700'), at the base of Mt. Baker, is an ideal camp for moderately strenuous overnight trips into this area. Continue past rockfall area on foot about 6 miles to the summer parking lot at Mt. Baker trailhead. Follow the trail, marked with blue metal tags on trees, except for the last ¼ mile; 2 miles to the cabin. Stable snow conditions are required for this hike as three avalanche chutes must be crossed on the trail. A short climb above the cabin brings one out of the forest at about 6000 feet for an outstanding view of the peak close above. Best in early or late winter when snow is stable.

Skyline Divide (6500') is an especially rewarding trip to the high, open ridgetop east of Glacier Creek; sweeping views of Baker and peaks to the north — Church, Tomyhoi, Winchester and many others. Approach is via Thompson Creek Road 3905, which forks east off Glacier Creek Road 1 mile from the highway. Drive to end of Road 3905, or wherever it is closed by snow, and follow the trail south, crossing Road 3907. The trail continues southeast, switchbacking up a steep hillside through heavy forest 1 ½ miles to the final steep, open slopes (about 5500') below the actual ridgetop. If snow is firm, one may continue 1-2 miles along the ridge.

Excelsior Ridge (5700') is an outstanding viewpoint just north of Mt. Baker Highway, with an unobstructed view of Tomyhoi, Shuksan, Baker, and other peaks. Park at plowed area about 10 miles east of Glacier opposite Excelsior trailhead. The trail route is easy to follow, although quite strenuous, as it switchbacks up the steep hillside to about 5200 feet at timberline. Snow must be stable for the ascent of the last 500 feet to ridgetop.

Wells Creek Road 403 forks south off Mt. Baker Highway almost opposite Excelsior trail. Road 403 and a spur, Road 403A, are closed to snowmobiles and other motorized vehicles in winter. The grade is gentle and it is a good route for beginners. Lovely Nooksack Falls are under the bridge which carries Road 403 across Nooksack River ½ mile from the highway. Mountain goats are sometimes seen along Wells Creek, north of Barometer Mountain. There is an open slope near here which avalanches onto the road; a good turnaround point. The left fork, Road 403A, also has good touring as it extends east of small Pinus Lake.

Welcome Pass (5200') is another viewpoint north of Mt. Baker Highway with views of Baker, Shuksan and Tomyhoi. Park at plowed area on highway about 1 mile west of Shuksan Highway Station. Follow

Road 4021, an old logging spur, about a mile. From its end ascend
north about a mile to the ridgetop above. Firm, stable snow is a must on
this route as it is steep and crosses several slide areas which come from
the open slopes below Welcome Pass.

   Tomyhoi Peak (7451') is occasionally climbed in winter for a 360
degree view of the peaks on both sides of the U. S.-Canadian border.
Drive about ½ mile east of Road 4021. Start where Twin Lakes Road
401 forks north off Baker Highway. (Parking will probably have to be
arranged elsewhere; this is a chain-up area and overnight parking is not
usually permited.) Follow road 3 miles to 3600 feet where Keep Kool
trail starts and continues through Gold Run Pass (5400') above. Descend to meadows below on north side of the pass (about 4400'), and
ascend north-northwest above Tomyhoi Lake to the broad south ridge
leading to the summit. There is no route free of avalanche hazard to the
peak; stable snow is essential for safety. The last 1000 feet steepens and
involves climbing snowy, icy rock with a steep descent into a notch near
the summit and short pitch to the top. Any part of the approach makes
an excellent outing; one need not go beyond Gold Run Pass for great
scenery.

   A truly grand loop trip is possible around Table Mountain above
Mt. Baker Ski Area and Mt. Baker Highway end. The scenery is
terrific, but the route has a high avalanche potential, especially off the
sides of Table Mountain. The route circles in a clockwise direction so
the snow traveler crosses the most hazardous slopes on the south side of
Table early in the day before they are warmed by the sun.

   Park at the ski area and ski or snowshoe to summer road end at Artist Point. From here head west and contour across the south side of
Table and continue to the north, descending slightly to the three **Chain
Lakes.** Traverse east just north of the largest lake — Iceberg — to Herman Saddle between Table Mountain and Mt. Herman to the northeast. Descend into the avalanche-prone valley containing Bagley Lake
and return to the ski area.

   An even more scenic and strenuous trip is past Table Mountain to
Ptarmigan Ridge, which leads west toward Mt. Baker, and Coleman
Pinnacle (6416'). Park at the ski area as for Chain Lakes, hike to Artist
Point and use the same precautions to traverse across the south side of
Table Mountain. Continue southwest along the broad, open crest of
Ptarmigan Ridge. The view of Baker ahead and Shuksan to the east is
awesome, with a vast array of smaller peaks north and east. There is
frequently a danger of slides on the steep slopes above timberline. A
good turnaround is Rainbow Glacier, 4 miles from Table Mountain.
Coleman Pinnacle, 2 miles beyond this point, is an easy ascent and a

better view for those with the strength and time to make the extra distance and elevation.

A challenging traverse from the end of **Mt. Baker Highway via Swift Creek** south to Baker Hot Spring and **Baker Lake** can be made when avalanche conditions are minimal. Much of the route is in the narrow Swift Creek valley; avalanche chutes cross the valley in several places. Generally the trail will be obscured by deep snow and routefinding must be by correlation of map with terrain. Park at the ski area, continue to Austin Pass and follow the trail route toward Lake Ann and Swift Creek and descend into a bowl southeast of Austin Pass. Follow the bowl and traverse southwest instead of climbing over the ridge east to Lake Ann. Continue descending southwest, with a steep 200-foot step into Swift Creek Basin. Follow the trail along Swift Creek, keeping an eye on possible avalanche chutes, to Baker Hot Spring and Road 3816, 6 miles from Austin Pass. It is another 5 miles to Baker Lake and usual winter road end. A special attraction is soaking tired muscles in the hot spring with snow all around. Transportation must be arranged in advance for the return drive. A tour to Lake Ann is also excellent, with good views of both Shuksan and Baker.

Two spur roads in valley bottoms lead east from Mt. Baker Highway toward Hannegan Pass and the north side of Mt. Shuksan. Both **North Fork Nooksack Road 404** and **Hannegan Road 402** are closed to snowmobiles and other motorized vehicles in winter. Turn off Mt. Baker Highway ¼ mile east of Skuksan Highway Station on Road 402, which is plowed 200 feet to a parking area. These roads are suitable for beginners and have good views of Mt. Shuksan and Mt. Sefrit. North Fork Nooksack Road runs east 2 miles where Hannegan Road forks left, then it continues another 3 miles at a very gentle grade toward Shuksan's glacier-hung north side. Hannegan Road is somewhat steeper and climbs toward Hannegan Pass, the last mile of this road, and Hannegan trail, are particularly subject to avalanching and are hazardous.

MAPS

Topographic

Silverton	(15-minute)	Lake Shannon	(15-minute)
Granite Falls	(15-minute)	Marblemount	(15-minute)
Hamilton	(15-minute)	Diablo Dam	(7½-minute)
Mt. Baker	(15-minute)	Ross Dam	(7½-minute)
Mt. Shuksan	(15-minute)	Old Stillaguamish	(30-minute)

U.S. Forest Service
Mt. Baker - Snoqualmie National Forest

Other
North Cascades National Park
The North Central Cascades; pictorial relief map by Richard A. Pargeter

DESTINATION	Elevation: Highest or Starting (+)	Elevation Gain	Miles: Round Trip or One Way (*)	Time	Map on Page
Mt. Pilchuck	5,324	2,500	5	6-8 hours	96
Schweitzer Road 3015	1,200+	optional	optional	optional	96
Mallardy Ridge Road 3034	3,500	2,200	8-9	8-10 hours	96
Kelcema Lake	3,182	1,600	10	5-10 hours	97
Helena Peak	5,401	3,800	14	12-14 hours	97
Devils Peak	5,453	3,800	10	10-12 hours	97
Coal Creek Road 3006	2,500	1,000	6-8	8-10 hours	97
Perry Creek Road 3010	1,700+	optional	optional	optional	97
Clear Creek Road 3210	600+	optional	optional	optional	97
Kennedy Hot Spring (from road end)	3,275	1,000	12	2-3 days	98
Suiattle Road 345	165+	optional	optional	optional	98
Green Mtn. (from Road 345)	6,500	5,300	12-14	12 hours or 2 days	98
Gold Mtn. Road 3204	625+	optional	optional	optional	97
Finney Creek Shelter	1,300	1,000	10	6-8 hours or 2 days	100
Bacon Creek Road 3717	365+	optional	optional	optional	101
Sourdough Mtn.	6,000	5,000	13-15	2-3 days	102
Dillard Point Lookout	2,400	1,250	4-5	5-6 hours	103
Schrieber's Meadows (from Baker Lake Highway)	3,500	2,113	12	5-6 hours	103
Koma Kulshan Guard Station	850+	optional	optional	optional	103
Anderson Creek Road 3721	500+	optional	optional	optional	103
Sandy Creek Road 3707	1,000+	optional	optional	optional	103
Baker Hot Spring (from Baker Lake)	1,400	700	12	8-10 hours or 2 days	103
Marten Lake Road	1,400+	optional	optional	optional	103
Kulshan Cabin (from rockfall cliff)	4,700	3,200	16	2-3 days	104
Skyline Divide	6,500	5,000	8	10-12 hours or 2 days	104
Excelsior Ridge	5,700	3,800	6	8 hours	104
Wells Creek Road 403	2,500	700	6	5-8 hours	104
Welcome Pass	5,200	3,200	6	6-8 hours	104
Tomyhoi Peak	7,451	5,400	14	3 days	104
Chain Lakes Loop	5,300	1,000	8	8-10 hours	104
Ptarmigan Ridge	6,000	1,700	14	10 hours or 2 days	104
Mt. Baker Highway via Swift Creek to Baker Lake	4,700	400 3,700 (loss)	12*	2 days	104, 103
North Fork Nooksack Road 404	2,700+	optional	optional	optional	104
Hannegan Road 402	2,700+	optional	optional	optional	104

Chapter 12

LEAVENWORTH, ENCHANTMENTS, AND U. S. 97 NORTH OF INGALLS CREEK

The mountain setting of the small town of Leavenworth needs little description. The business community has widely publicized the scenic attractions, as well as the city's redecorating project. For many years it has sponsored national and international ski jumping competition.

In addition to the rugged heights of the Enchantments of the Stuart range, there are many miles of snow-covered roads with gentle grades in deep, sheltered valleys. The forest varies from cedars, maples and cottonwood along streams to storm-twisted alpine tamarack, whitebark pine and alpine fir on ridgetops. This is deep snow country, with consequent avalanche hazard on steep slopes. Ironically one can dodge avalanches in Ingalls, Icicle and Tumwater canyons in winter, and beware of rattlesnakes in the same places in summer.

The air is still free of smog in this area. East of Leavenworth smoke and haze increase rapidly. But to the west the air is clearer; Puget Sound smog does not seem to drift through Stevens Pass to befoul the atmosphere as it does in the area east of Snoqualmie Pass.

Southwest of Leavenworth is **Icicle Ridge** (7029'), an exceptional vantage for Mt. Stuart and the Enchantments as well as the surrounding deep canyons. Avalanche danger is slight although the approach is long. Turn south off U. S. 2 on Icicle Road at the west outskirts of Leavenworth. The Icicle Ridge trail begins 1 ½ miles from U. S. 2

slightly south of the bridge across the Wenatchee River. Follow the trail up switchbacks on moderate slopes. The forest is thin and allows views of the surroundings. At 4 miles (4500') camp at a spring which is hard to find under deep snow, or continue ¾ mile farther to the actual ridgecrest at 5200 feet. There are groves of whitebark pine for camp shelter from here on. The ridgetop provides a nearly level crest for easy traveling, with the high point 4 ½ miles west. Rainier appears and the mountain scenery is magnificent.

The **Icicle Creek Road 2451** begins beyond the last residences about 4 miles from U. S. 2 and extends 15-20 miles or more, as logging roads are pushed farther into the headwaters of this stream. Side roads fork off in both directions, offering gentle terrain for touring and snowshoeing. The Icicle cascades among immense granite boulders, with peaks above on both sides of the canyon.

Snow Creek trail forks left (south) near what is usually the end of the plowed road. In winters of light snow the road is often open to and beyond Eightmile Creek Road 2412, 6 miles west of Snow Creek. Icicle Road is used by so many snowmobilers that trail breaking is seldom a problem for foot travelers.

Nada Lake (4950'), **Snow Lakes** (5400'), and the **Enchantment Lakes** (7000'+) can be reached via the Snow Creek trail, the most popular access route. The trail climbs steadily in 5 miles to Nada Lake, and 2 miles farther to Snow Lake. There are two avalanche areas to cross on this route; beware of snow conditions on the slopes above. Camp can be made at either of these lakes.

The most outstanding scenery is beyond and above Snow Lakes. Use the south shore of upper Snow Lake as the route to the inlet stream and follow generally the right (north) side to the basin 800 feet above. Avoid avalanche hazard off Temple Ridge to the right, as well as unstable snow on any open, steep slope. About 7000 feet the upper Enchantment Lakes Basin opens out with Prusik Peak to the right, Little Annapurna and McClellan Peak on the left, and a snow-covered lake in each hollow. Truly this is one of the most spectacular spots in the Cascades. Little Annapurna, McClellan, and Enchantment Peak (8520'), just west of Prusik, can be climbed from Enchantment Basin.

About 6 miles west of Snow Creek, Eightmile Creek Road 2412 forks south off Icicle Road. At time of writing the road extends about 5 miles, ending on the north side of Cannon Mountain. A spur to Eightmile Lake is planned. When Icicle Road is free of snow and one can drive to Eightmile Road, the several lakes and viewpoints are well suited to skis. The fast and rather effortless 3-mile glide down Eightmile Road makes possible one-day trips to several lakes.

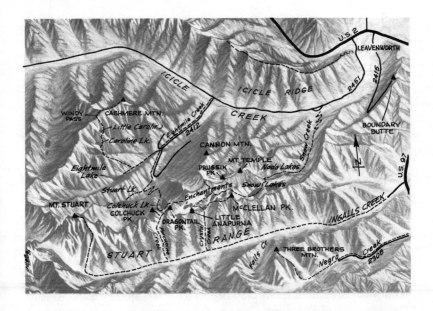

Camp can be made at the fork at Eightmile and Mountaineer Creeks, 3 ½ miles from Icicle Road, or at the lake which is the objective. The usual avalanche warning is very valid for this area. All these deep canyons may have snow which is absolutely safe from sliding in the valley bottoms and still be menaced by large slides from unstable slopes above.

Stuart Lake (5064') is reached via Mountaineer Creek trail about 5½ miles from Eightmile Road. The trail goes through heavy timber in places with some switchbacks. Massive slides from the north have wiped out the forest beyond Colchuck Lake trail fork, about 3 miles from Eightmile Road. The lake is surrounded by timber beneath a serrated ridge on the left, with Stuart's ice-sheathed north side beyond.

To reach **Colchuck Lake** (5570'), turn left on trail about 3 miles from Eightmile Road. The summer trail is steep and rough and the way may not be obvious. The forest is dense and the route wanders back and forth from bench to bench on an otherwise steep hillside. Dragontail and Colchuck Peaks rise impressively high above the lake with long open slopes which avalanche onto the lake; the ridge on the west side of the lake is not swept by slides. The long slope north of Dragontail Peak has been used in spring as access to the Enchantments.

Eightmile Lake (4641') is about 3 miles from Eightmile Road. The trail, or perhaps by now, road, forks right and climbs up into Eightmile Creek valley, which is actually a tributary to Mountaineer Creek. The setting is not as spectacular as that of the other lakes, but still lovely, with ridges and summits rising to over 7000 feet on either side.

The 1 ½-mile summer route to **Lake Caroline** (6190') over the righthand ridge is a vast winter avalanche slope just east of Eightmile Lake. Pick a route through forest east of this open area if there is any question of unstable snow; under safe conditions downhill skis and bindings make it an enjoyable run. Lake Caroline and Little Caroline are at the head of Pioneer Creek in the shallow valley north of Eightmile. Cashmere Mountain rises high above the lakes, to the northeast. Tamarack trees flourish in the rolling area around the lakes.

Cashmere Mountain (8501') is an enjoyable spring climb, up either the west ridge or the gully between it and a lower peak to the east. The upper west ridge near the summit is usually traversed on the north side as several rock towers call for strenuous rock climbing. The slopes and gullies are steep and unstable snow creates an extreme avalanche hazard.

At the northwest edge of Leavenworth, south of the ski jumping hill, **Tumwater Mountain Road 2450** begins its climb up the "back" side of the ridge east of Tumwater Canyon. Ski or snowshoe it as far as desired for a fine view out over the local area. From the ridgetop or the summit of Tumwater Mountain (4500') the view is outstanding: Tumwater Canyon below, Icicle Ridge beyond, and distant peaks.

Cross Wenatchee River east of Leavenworth on U. S. 2 and turn south on **Mountain Home Road 2415.** In about 7 miles the road reaches **Boundary Butte** (3168') on the ridge south of Leavenworth. The view of the town and the Enchantments peaks is outstanding. The road climbs from orchards through pine and fir forest, beside a massive section of lateral moraine boulders of the most recent Icicle Glacier, to the viewpoint above. Tour as far as time and energy permit.

Highway 97 forks south from U. S. 2 about 5 miles east of Leavenworth. A number of roads and trails which are interesting winter trips may be reached from this highway. Six miles south of U. S. 2, across from Ingalls Creek Lodge, turn west on secondary road 1 ½ miles to **Ingalls Creek trail** at dead end. Ingalls Creek heads on Ingalls Peak about 15 miles west, runs east past Mt. Stuart and drains streams from the south side of the Enchantments, the eastern part of the Stuart range. Elevation ranges from 1853 feet at trailhead to 4800 feet at the foot of Mt. Stuart. Since the trail stays on the north side of the creek for its entire length there are no difficult stream crossings. The forest changes from some old Douglas fir at the start, with maple, cottonwood and cedar along the stream, to lodgepole pine beyond Crystal Creek, alpine fir and others below Stuart, and alpine tamarack near Ingalls Lake.

Avalanches fall from the slopes on the north, especially between the 4-6 mile points — a regular "avalanche alley" — and again off Stuart. These well-defined chutes are quite obvious. A wooden cross at 5 ½ miles marks the grave of a trapper killed in a January 1928 slide. Water is available and sheltered camp spots abound. Beware of camping in open areas with good views; they may be avalanche chutes.

Skis or snowshoes are equally efficient on the trail, although novices on skis may have trouble skiing down the switchback sections. Skiers will have less trouble than snowshoers hanging on steep sidehills high above the stream where the trail ledge has been snowed over smooth.

There are side trails and possible routes not described in detail. One is Mill Creek trail which forks north 3 ½ miles up the trail and goes over a minor ridge in several miles, without much avalanche hazard. Falls Creek trail forks left at 5 ½ miles, crosses Ingalls Creek and goes to Falls Creek Pass west of Three Brothers. Avalanche hazard in upper valley.

Probably of greatest interest are the peaks along the south edge of the Enchantments area to the north. Crystal Creek, 7 ¾ miles up the trail, gives access to the upper Enchantment Lakes at Enchantment Pass (7100'). Stay on the east side of the stream. The 2000 feet above the trail is fairly steep, through open forest including some ponderosa pine and Douglas fir. The grade gentles as an area of immense boulders is reached, with the short, level valley just beyond. If there is unstable snow above, turn back, as the smooth walls of **Little Annapurna** (8436') on the left and **McClellan Peak** (8364'), right, feed slides onto the area. The last 500 feet to Enchantment Pass are steep, with no forest protection.

From the pass Crystal Lake is in the hollow left. Pick a route west up to the slopes of Little Annapurna, then south to the summit. This is an exceptional viewpoint for an outstanding area. If there is any unstable snow on Little Annapurna or McClellan Peak, turn back.

McClellan Peak can be climbed from Enchantment Pass also, but there is some steep scrambling near the top. Ascend southeast from the pass, circling toward the south side near the top. Carry rope, crampons and ice ax.

Dragontail Peak (8850') is the highest in the Enchantments and second to Stuart in this area. Excellent views from the gentle summit and nearby ridges. Follow Ingalls Creek trail 9 miles; camp can be made at about 4100 feet. Ascend directly north up the hillside, following an unnamed creek just east of Porcupine Creek, and enter the valley above with sheer Dragontail ridge to the left (west). Watch for unstable snow; the valley is moderate in slope and the greatest hazard will be snow sloughing off the side ridges.

The 7000-foot peaks south of Ingalls Creek are soon surmounted and Rainier appears. Snowshoes or skis may be left at the 8500-foot notch east of the summit, where one gets the first view of the Enchantments. Scramble 300 feet left to the summit. The view includes Mountaineer Creek valley and Colchuck Lake below, plus more distant peaks north, Rainier south, and Stuart to the west.

Colchuck Peak (8705') is the summit immediately west of Dragontail and directly above Colchuck Lake. Camp near the 9-mile marker on Ingalls Creek trail. Climb north up hillside and angle slightly west, following Porcupine Creek into valley directly west of Dragontail Ridge. Avalanche hazard is greater off side ridges than down the moderately sloping valley, although massive slides do sweep each of these open valleys at times. If snow is unstable, turn back; the final 500 feet or so of Colchuck is somewhat steep and avalanches directly down the valley.

At 7600 feet the valley divides directly below the peak at a monolith resembling an Easter Island statue. Take the right (east) fork toward Banshee Pass (8000') between Colchuck and Dragontail. Ascend to the summit from here or pick a route which starts lower. The slope eases just below the two summits, of which the western is higher. Again the view is outstanding, but is more of Stuart, Argonaut and the more distant Cascade peaks than the Enchantments.

Mt. Stuart (9418') is the spectacular high point of the Stuart Range. Its jagged granite summit can be seen from I-90 east of Cle Elum, and more distantly from I-90 west of Moses Lake. Often approached but seldom climbed in winter, it is a worthy objective for the winter mountaineer. It is remote from roads, and requires rope, ice ax and crampons; its upper slopes are steep and avalanche hazard extreme unless snow is stable. The north side has been successfully ascended in late winter after warm temperature had released avalanches, and then cool, clear weather settled in for several days.

Ski or snowshoe Ingalls Creek trail 12 miles to the base of Stuart. Crystal Creek, at 7 ¾ miles, makes a good first night's camp. Do not camp in open meadows at the base of Stuart; they are "open" due to avalanches down the long gullies of the mountain. Climb west beside the gully opposite Turnpike Creek leading toward the false summit. If there is unstable snow, turn back. Slopes are steep enough that snowshoes or skis are left behind about 500 feet above Ingalls Creek. Snow should be firm enough to kick steps in without snowshoes or skis. Climb over false summit and follow well left of the ridge to the summit above; cornices overhang north side on the right. Below both summit and false summit are lee slopes which may have deep accumulations of wind-blown snow which can form wind slab, a most unstable form of snow.

The view is indescribable, extending from Baker to Adams and St. Helens, plus all the peaks and valleys below and between the three distant volcanic peaks. However, fatigue may dim the visual enjoyment somewhat — it is a long, hard three-day pull to achieve this point. Someday someone is going to ski up the North Fork Teanaway, over Turnpike or Long's Pass, climb the mountain and return down the gentle road approach from the south.

DESTINATION	Elevation: Highest or Starting (+)	Elevation Gain	Miles: Round Trip or One Way (*)	Time	Map on Page
Icicle Ridge	7,029	5,800	17	2-3 days	90, 111
Icicle Creek Road 2451	1,300+	optional	optional	optional	90, 111
Nada Lake	4,950	3,650	10	6-8 hours	111
Snow Lakes	5,400	4,100	14	2 days	111
Enchantment Lakes	7,000	5,700	18	3 days	111
Stuart Lake	5,064	3,064	17	2-3 days	111
Colchuck Lake	5,570	3,570	16	2-3 days	111
Eightmile Lake	4,641	2,641	12	1-2 days	111
Lake Caroline	6,190	4,190	15	2-3 days	111
Cashmere Mtn.	8,501	6,501	20	2-3 days	111
Tumwater Mtn. Road 2450	1,500+	optional	optional	optional	90
Mountain Home Road 2415	1,200+	optional	optional	optional	111
Boundary Butte	3,168	2,000	14	10-12 hours or 2 days	111
Ingalls Creek Trail	1,953+	optional	optional	optional	111
Little Annapurna	8,436	6,500	23	3-4 days	111
McClellan Peak	8,364	6,400	23	3-4 days	111
Dragontail Peak	8,850	6,800	25	3-4 days	111
Colchuck Peak	8,705	6,800	25	3-4 days	111
Mt. Stuart	9,418	7,500	28	4-5 days	111

MAPS

Topographic

Leavenworth	(15-minute)
Liberty	(15-minute)
Mt. Stuart	(15-minute)
Chiwaukum	(15-minute)

U.S. Forest Service
Wenatchee National Forest

Other
The North Central Cascades; pictorial relief map by Richard A. Pargeter

Chapter 13

ENTIAT, LAKE CHELAN, NORTH CASCADES HIGHWAY, PASAYTEN WILDERNESS AREA

To describe terrain, weather and snow conditions, and forest of this vast area would require many pages. Elevations vary from 1100 feet at Lake Chelan to 8876 feet on Silver Star Mountain; vegetation changes from sagebrush at low elevations near the Columbia River through ponderosa pine to fir and cedar in deep, moist valleys near the Cascade Crest, to timberline species of whitebark pine, alpine fir, and larch east of the crest; the high, treeless, rounded ridges near the Canadian border in the Pasayten Wilderness Area contrast with the jagged spires of the Liberty Bell group at Washington Pass.

Generally snow and weather conditions are similar to those east of the Cascade range farther south. However, the temperatures are coldest of any area described in this guide, as subzero air from Canada often slips into this area; be prepared with adequate clothing and equipment.

It is a long drive from the Puget Sound cities, and there are consequently fewer people on the roads and trails. A few skiers have toured into the Lyman Lake and Pasayten areas for stays of several weeks. Others on snowshoes have hiked the North Cascades Highway from Diablo to Mazama, crossed from Darrington to Lucerne via Suiattle and Cloudy Passes, and from the Entiat to Lucerne through Milham Pass, as well as a group which approached Dome Peak via the West Fork Agnes, and made a brief sortie to high peaks north of Dome. Even with ideal weather and snow conditions, these routes are as rugged as the scenery they pass through.

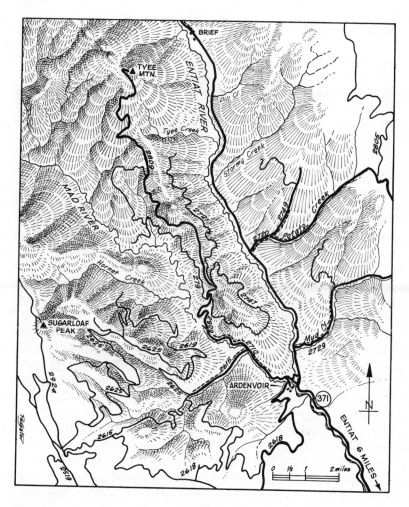

Entiat

The Entiat River valley has miles of road suitable for ski touring and snowshoeing as well as more alpine ridges and peaks. Mills Canyon Road 2924 climbs south from Entiat Road 317 about 3 miles from U. S. 97. Other roads fork off it, some leading to distant viewpoints such as Chumstick Mountain overlooking Wenatchee valley to the south. However, most people on foot will be satisfied with shorter tours overlooking Entiat valley. Most logging roads are used extensively by snowmobilers.

At Ardenvoir roads lead to both sides of the valley. Road 2710 starts west beside Mad River, then forks south, as Road 2615, toward

Sugarloaf Peak (5840'). Road 2809 climbs from Mad River to the ridge between Mad and Entiat Rivers and ends at Tyee Mountain (6688'), with an excellent view of the high peaks in the head of the Entiat, and the awesome burn of the 1970 forest fires.

Mud Creek Road 2729 and **Potato Creek Road 2720** follow streams up the east side of the valley, leaving **Entiat Road** north of Ardenvoir. The most ambitious trip is to the end of Entiat Road and by trail to Snowbrushy Creek, continuing to Milham Pass (6663') through the Chelan Mountains, then descending Emerald Park Creek to Domke Lake and **Lucerne** on Lake Chelan. A retired valley pioneer skied this route in the 1920's.

The route climbs steadily along the Entiat Road then up Snowbrushy Creek with little slide danger until near the pass. This will require 4-5 days, depending on how far one can drive on Entiat Road, which normally is open to Brief, about 10 miles beyond Ardenvoir.

Enjoyable trips are possible on the snow-covered road, without attempting the crossing of Milham Pass. A tour through the burned section beyond Brief should cause any outdoorsman to pause and reflect on the destructiveness of forest fires.

Road 298 up Lake Creek leads to the Chelan Mountain crest just beyond **Shady Pass** (6000'). There are superb views from this divide between Entiat valley and Lake Chelan in its deep trench to the northeast. The ridge continues about 6 miles to Junior Point overlook (6676'), but nearly equal views may be had by following west, either on the road or ridgetop, toward Big Hill (6800').

The ridgetop route continues about 8 miles to **Pyramid Peak** (8245'), with several climbs and descents over minor points. Any unstable snow on the high, open slopes near Pyramid should dictate a retreat. The ridgetop is exposed to wind and storm, but has many sheltering groves of trees for camp sites. On that perfect, clear, winter day, the view from Pyramid is excellent.

Lake Chelan below leads one's gaze to the peaks of the Stehekin. Beyond nearby Cardinal Peak rise the Maude-Seven Fingered Jack-Fernow group, with Glacier and Rainier in the distance. A loop trip may be made by descending southwest into Pyramid Creek to North Fork Entiat, and return.

Lake Chelan

Lake Chelan is a scenic highlight, although the interminable boat ride is a frustration to those who intend to hike and tour upon arrival at lake's end destinations. Usually deer and goats are visible along the

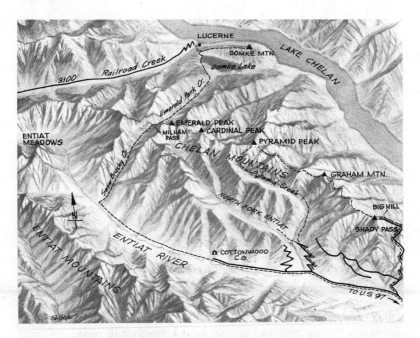

way, most frequently on the south-facing slopes along the shore, and in late February or early March one might see bald eagles. Bring binoculars for viewing wildlife. The winter ferry schedule is limited to Monday, Wednesday, and Friday, leaving Chelan at 8:00 a.m. and Twenty-five Mile Creek at 9:30 a.m., arriving at Stehekin about noon, and return to Chelan about 5:00 p.m. At present the Lutheran Church facility at Holden, 12 miles from Lucerne, operates a winter schedule, including a snow cat for transportation, which can be arranged by contacting Holden Village.

The special attractions are the miles of open slope around Lyman Lake (5587'), ideal for touring to high points with views of Bonanza, Glacier, and the many other peaks, then the downhill run back to camp in the grove near the lake.

It is 8 miles from **Holden to Lyman Lake,** where some sheltering forest and a large expanse of gentle terrain make an excellent campspot. In the past the cabin at the lake was open to the public, but unfortunately this is no longer the case. It may be necessary to camp part way in, as the late arrival in Holden after boat and snow vehicle transport makes the first day quite short. Avalanches off the shoulder of Bonanza Peak sweep entirely across Hart Lake at times. However, the greatest avalanche hazard is the 1000-foot climb out of the valley beside Crown Point Falls. Most parties use the trail route. This unavoidable slope is swept by avalanches at times; stable snow is necessary here. Late winter — April — is the best time for a visit.

Several tours and hikes radiate from Lyman Lake. **Cloudy Pass** (6438') is a short mile northeast. The vast open slope of **North Star Mountain** (8068') not only has a superb view, but often excellent downhill skiing as well. Touring south of the lake is more limited, but skiing on Lyman Glacier can be as rewarding as the ascent of **Chiwawa Mountain** (8459'), just above it. (Bring ice ax and rope for climbing Chiwawa.)

Summit views are of the nearby peaks of the Dome group, Bonanaza, Glacier, Baker to the north, and Rainier beyond the fluted "wall" of Fortress Mountain.

Occasionally a party makes an early or late season traverse through this area from **Darrington to Holden.** The distance depends upon how far the Suiattle River Road can be driven from Darrington; the avalanche potential is extreme, but the challenge is there and the scenery exceptional. One party was successful in mid-December of a light-snowfall year, although enduring four days of rain and one of snow. Image Lake was bypassed in favor of Miners Creek trail as the first avalanche debris observed at that trail junction had obviously come from the slopes below the lake. A cabin near Glacier Peak Mines (5500') was used. Gentle slopes west of Suiattle Pass (5983') were pleasant after the long climb out of the Suiattle. A fast, heart-in-throat traverse across a steep, loose north slope brought the party to Cloudy Pass (6438'). Avalanches roared unseen in the murk the next morning during the descent past Crown Point, and the entire day was spent slogging wearily in wet, heavy snow. The lights of Holden provided a cheery welcome as the sodden trio arranged warm, dry accommodations, their first in several days.

Domke Mountain (4100') is an enjoyable hike or tour from Lucerne, on Lake Chelan. The 2½-mile trail ascends to the summit for a good view of the lake and surrounding peaks.

Stehekin valley is the beginning of several hikes or tours, some easy and others strenuous. Heavy snowfall, alpine peaks and miles of steep hillsides create considerable avalanche hazard. Early or late winter is best in this area. Stehekin Road is plowed 8 miles beyond Stehekin.

A tour on the road or a walk beside the river may be all one has time or energy to do. Check with Park Service before touring into the back-country. The road extends about 17 miles past High Bridge, nearly to Horseshoe Basin. The only spur leads to the airstrip and slightly beyond Company Creek. **Coon Lake** (2149') is a short hike above the road, east of High Bridge.

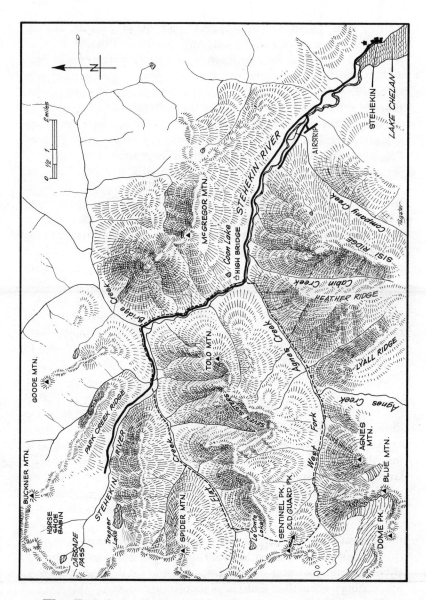

West Fork Agnes has been visited in winter, within sight of Dome Peak. Follow the trail route along Agnes Creek from High Bridge. The route climbs very gently the 6 miles to the junction with the West Fork (2400'), where there is a bridge across the main Agnes. The West Fork Agnes is nearly level for 3-4 miles, as cottonwoods and aspen mingle with conifers. At about 2500 feet the forest ends and brush or avalanche debris begins. The creek descends here in a series of cascades, and one quickly gains elevation to 3400 feet. Any slide hazard should dictate a retreat. The view to the east includes McGregor Mountain, Agnes Peak and Lyall Ridge across the main Agnes. The cascading section is ascended on the south of the creek, where a last patch of forest appears. Emerging from the forest, one can see Dome Peak and Spire Point.

Old Guard and Sentinel Peaks, north of Dome Peak, were approached via Flat Creek and climbed during clear April weather. Previous warm days had stabilized much loose snow, and cold temperatures at night provided firm footing in the morning. However, warm daytime temperatures caused many small slides in the afternoon. By carefully observing this pattern, the group avoided being caught by sliding snow, but the potential danger was higher than most persons will accept. Where the canyon narrows and forest ends below Le Conte Glacier, it is apparent that there is no avalanche-free route to these peaks.

A loop trip was completed by descending a large avalanche gully west of Old Guard into West Fork Agnes in early morning, so as not to interfere with the afternoon snow slides down the same chute. This route is included mainly to record that it was done. But, like the winter ascent of Willis Wall, it is not one to be blundered into uninformed as to the possible hazards.

North Cascades Highway

The North Cascades Highway has caused an increased interest in the Methow valley, east-side approach to Washington Pass (5477'). Groups tour or snowshoe the route, and an avalanche study group regularly skis in and out from their cabin at the pass. In winter the snow and ice-hung peaks and ridges are indescribably beautiful.

The 2-mile section of highway east of Washington Pass overlook has the greatest avalanche hazard. Some of the many slide paths in this section deposit piles of snow a hundred yards or so wide on the roadway. By traversing from west to east, this area may be descended quickly, minimizing the length of time one is exposed to danger.

The most spectacular single avalanche pile is below the Early Winters Spires; it fills the road grade so that it is an unbroken, steep slope at that point. Some parties work their way down the forested slope due east of the pass rather than cross this slide path, which also saves walking about a mile of road where it makes a long loop south of the Liberty Bell group of peaks.

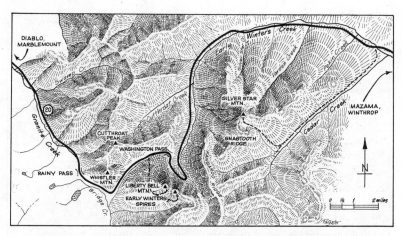

There are many other avalanche chutes which pile up on the high-way off the south and west sides of Whistler Peak, and others along Granite Creek. The highway west of Diablo was closed by avalanches for portions of 30 days or so in the winter of 1971-72. One wonders why a route so menaced by snowslides was ever built. From winter road end east of **Diablo** to near Mazama in the **Methow** is 55 miles, with high points at Rainy Pass and Washington Pass.

Winter ascents have been made on **Liberty Bell Peak** (7500') from the south notch, and **South Early Winters Spire** (7807') via the snow- or ice-filled southwest gully. The summit views are of the widest extent of the Washington Cascades, with Silver Star in the east, and peaks from Mt. Baker in the north to Rainier and Stuart in the south, running one behind the other in spectacular profusion. Either foot or snowmobile transportation the 12 miles from winter road end near Mazama is rugged. There is no avalanche-free approach to these peaks; snow must be stable for any winter ascents in this area.

Cedar Creek is an access route menaced by avalanches leading to a group of high snow-embossed rocky summits crowned by **Silver Star Mountain** (8876'). The trail up Cedar Creek starts about 1 mile west of winter road end on the North Cascades Highway 2 miles west of Mazama. Follow it through heavy forest about 8 miles, and at 4700 feet fork right (west) and follow a tributary which descends from the largest southeast basin between Snagtooth Ridge on the south and the east ridge of Silver Star.

The basin is swept by avalanches. Ascend steepening snow as the main gully leads from the head of the basin to the summit. The view is similar to that from Liberty Bell, except that the Liberty Bell group is in the foreground.

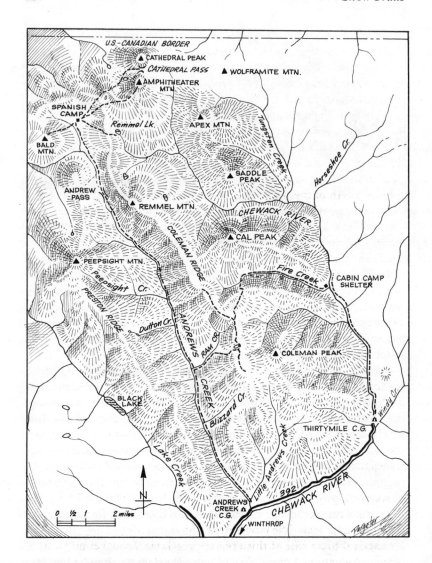

Pasayten Wilderness Area

The vast expanse of the Pasayten Wilderness Area is attractive for several-day expeditions, although many difficulties are inherent in such an outing. It is a full day's travel by car to reach Winthrop in the Methow or Tonasket in the Okanogan, from Puget Sound cities. One must plan the logistics carefully, including securing a Wilderness Permit. This is an area where temperatures can plummet below zero and blizzard conditions set in overnight; a base camp shelter must be solid and well stocked with food. Groups from the temperate Puget Sound area are sometimes rudely introduced to the results of low temperatures: though the party is well equipped and clothed for outdoors comfort they may encounter a problem if the engine and battery have been overlooked, and the car refuses to start after sitting for several days in such frigid surroundings.

A choice objective is **Spanish Camp** at the head of Chewack River, reached most easily via Andrews Creek, a tributary of the Chewack. It is 22 miles from Winthrop to Andrews Creek trailhead (2975'), and feasibility of the trip depends upon how far the Chewack Road is plowed north of the town, and whether any of it is closed to the public during the week (some of the roads are plowed for logging access).

Andrews Creek trail is broad and climbs at a gentle grade to Andrew Pass (6400'), then continues across the broad, gentle basin of Spanish Creek to 6600-foot Spanish Camp at the north side. About 15 miles from Chewack Road there is (at time of writing) a cabin which is open to the public in winter. The site is near timberline, with the groves of trees giving way to the continuous white of rounded divides between stream and the higher summits near and far. The location is ideal as a base camp for day trips to the surrounding high points, or for touring above timberline.

To the southwest rises the dome of **Bald Mountain** (7931'), reached either by the trail route, or by touring on a divide to the south. **Amphitheater Mountain** (8358') is an easy climb also, and both make excellent viewpoints of the surrounding area, including Cathedral Peak to the north, and beyond Remmel Mountain to the south. Other tours include the divide southeast from Spanish Camp toward Remmel.

Coleman Ridge, south of Remmel Mountain, on the east side of Andrews Creek, can be reached by Ram Creek trail, which forks east off Andrews Creek trail, or Fire Creek trail from Chewack River trail, providing one can drive up Chewack Road far enough to make it a practical approach. The view is excellent.

Several tours east of this area approach via Tonasket on U. S. 97, then to Loomis, and on up Toats Coulee Road, depending on how far it is free of snow. Windy Peak trail reaches **Windy Peak** (8334') in about 6 miles. This high point on the south rim of Horseshoe Basin, a large glacial cirque, has a view west to Cathedral, Peepsight, Remmel, and other peaks.

Farther east Iron Gate trail 361 also leads to **Horseshoe Basin,** following a ridge north, then east along the head of the basin. From a pass the trail descends slightly to the head of the basin, in about 5 miles.

Strength and time available determine the terminus of winter travel here. There are other possible routes, and avalanche hazard is minimal, with the exception of steep slopes such as Remmel's south and east sides. There are many miles of ridgetop — open, gentle, with wonderful views — which are safe to travel.

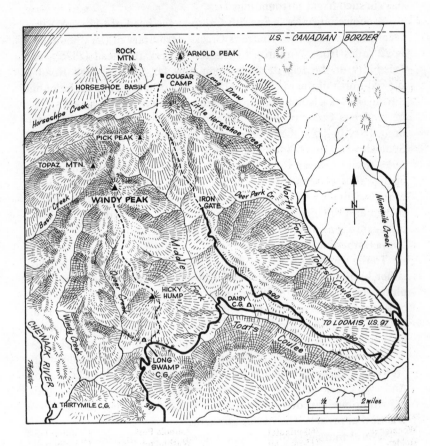

MAPS

U.S. Forest Service
Pasayten Wilderness
Okanogan National Forest
Wenatchee National Forest

Other
The North Central Cascades; pictorial relief map by Richard A. Pargeter

DESTINATION	Elevation: Highest or Starting (+)	Elevation Gain	Miles: Round Trip or One Way (*)	Time	Map on Page
Mud Creek Road 2729	1,650+	optional	optional	optional	117
Potato Creek Road 2720	1,800+	optional	optional	optional	117
Entiat Road to Lucerne (from 2,000')	6,663	4,663	24*	3-4 days	119
Shady Pass	6,000	4,000	15	8-10 hours or 2 days	119
Pyramid Peak	8,245	6,200+	32	4 days	119
Holden to Lyman Lake	5,587	2,400	16	2-3 days	98, 119
Cloudy Pass (from Lyman Lake)	6,438	850	2	3-4 hours	98
North Star Mtn.	8,068	2,600	4	4-5 hours	98
Chiwawa Mtn.	8,459	2,850	7	8-10 hours	98
Darrington to Holden (from Suiattle road end)	6,438	4,787	25*	5-6 days	98
Domke Mtn.	4,100	3,000	5	5-7 hours	119
Coon Lake	2,149	500	2½	3-4 hours	121
West Fork Agnes (to last trees)	2,500	1,000	23	5 days	121
Diablo to Methow (from Diablo turnoff)	5,477	4,900+	55*	4-6 days	123
Liberty Bell Peak (from Washington Pass)	7,500	2,050	2	6-8 hours	123
South Early Winters Spire (from Washington Pass)	7,807	2,330	2½	5-7 hours	123
Silver Star Mtn.	8,876	6,700	21	3 days	123
Spanish Camp	6,750	4,000	30	4-5 days	124
Bald Mtn.	7,931	1,200	3	4-6 hours	124
Amphitheater Mtn.	8,358	1,600	5	6-8 hours	124
Coleman Ridge	7,000	4,000	24	3-4 days	124
Windy Peak (from Toats Coulee Road)	8,334	2,834	14	8-12 hours or 2 days	126
Horseshoe Basin (from Toats Coulee Road)	7,200	1,200	14	8-12 hours or 2 days	126

MAPS

Topographic

Wenatchee	(60-minute)	Ashnola Pass	(7½-minute)
Holden	(15-minute)	Washington Pass	(7½-minute)
Lucerne	(15-minute)	Silver Star Mtn.	(7½-minute)
Horseshoe Basin	(15-minute)	Dome Peak	(7½-minute)
Glacier Peak	(15-minute)	Goode Mtn.	(7½-minute)
Remmel Mtn.	(7½-minute)	Cascade Pass	(7½-minute)
Horseshoe Basin	(7½-minute)	Agnes Mtn.	(7½-minute)
Coleman Ridge	(7½-minute)	Mt. Lyall	(7½-minute)
Bauerman Ridge	(7½-minute)	Mt. McGregor	(7½-minute)
Mt. Barney	(7½-minute)	Mazama	(7½-minute)
Stehekin	(7½-minute)		